SERMON
ON
THE MOUNT

Jen Wilkin

Lifeway Press®
Brentwood, Tennessee

EDITORIAL TEAM
LIFEWAY WOMEN
BIBLE STUDIES

Becky Loyd
Director, Lifeway Women

Tina Boesch
Manager

Chelsea Waack
Production Leader

Laura Magness
Content Editor

Tessa Morrell
Production Editor

Lauren Ervin
Graphic Designer

Published by Lifeway Press® • © 2024 Jen Wilkin

ISBN: 978-1-0877-8836-4

Item: 005842837

Dewey Decimal Classification: 226.9
Subject Headings: SERMON ON THE MOUNT \ CHRISTIAN LIFE \ BIBLE. N.T. MATTHEW 5-7

To order additional copies of this resource, order online at www.lifeway.com; write Lifeway Resources Customer Service: One Lifeway Plaza, Nashville, TN 37234-0113; fax order to 615.251.5933; or call toll-free 1.800.458.2772.

Printed in the United States of America

Lifeway Women Bible Studies

Lifeway Resources
200 Powell Place, Suite 100
Brentwood, TN 37027-7707

Cover Design: Stephen Crotts

Author is represented by Wolgemuth & Wilson, Inc.

Contents

ABOUT THE AUTHOR

Jen Wilkin is an author and Bible teacher from Dallas, Texas. She has organized and led studies for women in home, church, and parachurch contexts. Her passion is to see others become articulate and committed followers of Christ, with a clear understanding of why they believe what they believe, grounded in the Word of God. Jen is the author of *Ten Words to Live By: Delighting in and Doing What God Commands*, *Women of the Word*, *None Like Him*, *In His Image*, and Bible studies exploring the books of Genesis, Exodus, Hebrews, 1 Peter, and 1,2,3 John. You can find her at jenwilkin.net.

ABOUT THE GOSPEL COALITION

The Gospel Coalition is a fellowship of evangelical churches deeply committed to renewing our faith in the gospel of Christ and to reforming our ministry practices to conform fully to the Scriptures. We have become deeply concerned about some movements within traditional evangelicalism that seem to be diminishing the church's life and leading us away from our historic beliefs and practices. On the one hand, we are troubled by the idolatry of personal consumerism and the politicization of faith; on the other hand, we are distressed by the unchallenged acceptance of theological and moral relativism. These movements have led to the easy abandonment of both biblical truth and the transformed living mandated by our historic faith. We not only hear of these influences, we see their effects.

We have committed ourselves to invigorating churches with new hope and compelling joy based on the promises received by grace alone through faith alone in Christ alone. We believe that in many evangelical churches a deep and broad consensus exists regarding the truths of the gospel. Yet we often see the celebration of our union with Christ replaced by the age-old attractions of power and affluence, or by monastic retreats into ritual, liturgy, and sacrament. What replaces the gospel will never promote a mission-hearted faith anchored in enduring truth working itself out in unashamed discipleship eager to stand the tests of kingdom-calling and sacrifice. We desire to advance along the King's highway, always aiming to provide gospel advocacy, encouragement, and education so that current- and next-generation church leaders are better equipped to fuel their ministries with principles and practices that glorify the Savior and do good to those for whom He shed His life's blood.

We want to generate a unified effort among all peoples—an effort that is zealous to honor Christ and multiply His disciples, joining in a true coalition for Jesus. Such a biblically grounded and united mission is the only enduring future for the church. This reality compels us to stand with others who are stirred by the conviction that the mercy of God in Jesus Christ is our only hope of eternal salvation. We desire to champion this gospel with clarity, compassion, courage, and joy—gladly linking hearts with fellow believers across denominational, ethnic, and class lines.

Our desire is to serve the church we love by inviting all of our brothers and sisters to join us in an effort to renew the contemporary church in the ancient gospel of Christ so we truly speak and live for Him in a way that clearly communicates to our age. As pastors, we intend to do this in our churches through the ordinary means of His grace: prayer, ministry of the Word, baptism and the Lord's Supper, and the fellowship of the saints. We yearn to work with all who seek the lordship of Christ over the whole of life with unabashed hope in the power of the Holy Spirit to transform individuals, communities, and cultures.

In its Women's Initiatives, The Gospel Coalition aims for gospel renewal specifically among and through the women of the church. We desire to support the growth of women in faithfully studying and sharing the Scriptures; in actively loving and serving the church; and in spreading the gospel of Jesus Christ in all their callings. Women benefit from and contribute to The Gospel Coalition's resources in many ways—on the website, in conference settings, and in various publishing projects. We pray that, through the Women's Initiatives, Jesus will be glorified and the church will be strengthened.

FOREWORD: HOW SHOULD WE APPROACH GOD'S WORD?

OUR PURPOSE

The Bible study you are about to begin will teach you an important passage of the Bible in a way that will stay with you for years to come. It will challenge you to move beyond loving God with just your heart to loving Him with your mind. It will focus on answering the question, "What does the Bible say about God?" It will aid you in the worthy task of God-discovery.

You see, the Bible is not a book about self-discovery; it is a book about God-discovery. The Bible is God's declared intent to make Himself known to us. In learning about the character of God in Scripture, we *will* experience self-discovery, but it must not be the object of our study. The object must be God Himself.

This focus changes the way we study. We look first for what a passage can teach us about the character of God, allowing self-discovery to be the by-product of God-discovery. This is a much better approach because there can be no true knowledge of self apart from knowledge of God. So when I read the account of Jonah, I see first that God is just and faithful to His Word—He is faithful to proclaim His message to Nineveh no matter what. I see second that I, by contrast (and much like Jonah), am unjust to my fellow man and unfaithful to God's Word. Thus, knowledge of God leads to true knowledge of self, which leads to repentance and transformation. So are confirmed Paul's words in Romans 12:2 that we are transformed by the renewing of our minds.

Most of us are good at loving God with our hearts. We are good at employing our emotions in our pursuit of God. But the God who commands us to love with the totality of our hearts, souls, and strength also commands us to love Him with all of our minds. Because He only commands what He also enables His children to do, it must be possible for us to love Him well with our minds or He would not command it. I know you will bring your emotions to your study of God's Word, and that is good and right. But it is your mind I am jealous for. God intends for you to be a good student, renewing your mind and thus transforming your heart.

OUR PROCESS

Being a good student entails following good study habits. When we sit down to read, most of us like to read through a particular passage and then find a way to apply it to our everyday lives. We may read through an entire book of the Bible over a period of time, or we may jump around from place to place. I want to suggest a different approach, one that may not always yield immediate application, comfort, or peace, but one that builds over time a cumulative understanding of the message of Scripture.

READING IN CONTEXT AND REPETITIVELY

Imagine yourself receiving a letter in the mail. The envelope is handwritten, but you don't glance at the return address. Instead you tear open the envelope, flip to the second page, read two paragraphs near the bottom, and set the letter aside. Knowing that if someone bothered to send it to you, you should act on its contents in some way, you spend a few minutes trying to figure out how to respond to what the section you just read had to say. What are the odds you will be successful?

No one would read a letter this way. But this is precisely the way many of us read our Bibles. We skip past reading the "envelope"—*Who wrote this? To whom was it written? When was it written? Where was it written?*—and then try to determine the purpose of its contents from a portion of the whole. What if we took time to read the envelope? What if, after determining the context for its writing, we started at the beginning and read to the end? Wouldn't that make infinitely more sense?

In our study, we will take this approach to Scripture. We will begin by placing our text in its historical and cultural context. We will "read the envelope." Then we will read through the entire text so that we can better determine what it wants to say to us. We will read repetitively so that we might move through three critical stages of understanding: comprehension, interpretation, and application.

STAGE 1: COMPREHENSION

Remember the reading comprehension section on the SAT? Remember those long reading passages followed by questions to test your knowledge of what you had just read? The objective was to force you to read for detail. We are going to apply the same method to our study of God's Word. When we read for comprehension, we ask ourselves, *What does it say?* This is hard work. A person who *comprehends* the account of the six days of creation can tell you specifically what happened on each day. This is the first step toward being able to interpret and apply the story of creation to our lives.

STAGE 2: INTERPRETATION

While comprehension asks, *What does it say?*, interpretation asks, *What does it mean?* Once we have read a passage enough times to know what it says, we are ready to look into its meaning. A person who *interprets* the creation story can tell you why God created in a particular order or way. She is able to imply things from the text beyond what it says.

STAGE 3: APPLICATION

After doing the work to understand what the text says and what the text means, we are finally ready to ask, *How should it change me?* Here is where we draw on our God-centered perspective to ask three supporting questions:

- What does this passage teach me about God?
- How does this aspect of God's character change my view of self?
- What should I do in response?

A person who *applies* the creation story can tell us that because God creates in an orderly fashion, we, too, should live well-ordered lives. Knowledge of God gleaned through comprehension of the text and interpretation of its meaning can now be applied to my life in a way that challenges me to be different.

SOME GUIDELINES

It is vital to the learning process that you allow yourself to move through the three stages of understanding on your own, without the aid of commentaries or study notes. The first several times you read a passage, you will probably be confused. In our study together, not all the homework questions will have answers that are immediately clear to you. This is actually a good thing. If you are unsure of an answer, give it your best shot.

Allow yourself to feel lost, to dwell in the "I don't know." It will make the moment of discovery stick. We'll also expand our understanding in the small-group discussion and teaching time.

Nobody likes to feel lost or confused, but it is an important step in the acquisition and retention of understanding. Because of this, I have a few guidelines to lay out for you as you go through this study.

1. **Avoid all commentaries** until *comprehension* and *interpretation* have been earnestly attempted on your own. In other words, wait to read commentaries until after you have done the homework, attended small-group time, and listened to the teaching. And then, consult commentaries you can trust. Ask a pastor or Bible teacher at your church for suggested authors. I used the following commentaries and books in creating this study: *The Divine Conspiracy* by Dallas Willard, *The Message of the Sermon on the Mount* by John Stott, *An Exposition of the Sermon on the Mount* by Arthur W. Pink, and *Matthew, a Commentary* by F. Dale Bruner.

2. For the purposes of this study, **get a Bible without study notes.** Come on, it's just too easy to look at them. You know I'm right.

3. Though commentaries are initially off-limits, here are some **tools you should use:**

- **Cross-references.** These are the Scripture references in the margin or at the bottom of the page in your Bible. They point you to other passages that deal with the same topic or theme.

- **An English dictionary** to look up unfamiliar words. A good online dictionary is *merriam-webster.com.*

- **Other translations of the Bible.** We will use the English Standard Version (ESV) as a starting point, but you can easily consult other versions online. I recommend the Christian Standard Bible (CSB), New International Version (NIV), New American Standard Version (NASB), and New King James Version (NKJV). Reading more than one translation can expand your understanding of the meaning of a passage. Note: a paraphrase, such as *The Message*, can be useful but should be regarded as a commentary rather than a translation. They are best consulted after careful study of an actual translation.

- **A printed copy of the text,** double-spaced, so you can mark repeated words, phrases, or ideas. A complete copy of Matthew 5–7 is provided for you to mark at the back of this workbook.

STORING UP TREASURE

Approaching God's Word with a God-centered perspective, with context, and with care takes effort and commitment. It is study for the long-term. Some days your study may not move you emotionally or speak to an immediate need. You may not be able to apply a passage at all. But what if ten years from now, in a dark night of the soul, that passage suddenly opens up to you because of the work you have done today? Wouldn't your long-term investment be worth it?

In Matthew 13 we see Jesus begin to teach in parables. He tells seven deceptively simple stories that left His disciples struggling for understanding—dwelling in the "I don't know," if you will. After the last parable, He turns to them and asks, "Have you understood all these things?" (v. 51a). Despite their apparent confusion, they answer out of their earnest desire with, "Yes" (v. 51b). Jesus tells them that their newfound understanding makes them "like the owner of a house who brings out of his storeroom new treasures as well as old" (v. 52, NIV).

A storeroom, as Jesus indicated, is a place for keeping valuables over a long period of time for use when needed. Faithful study of God's Word is a means for filling our spiritual storerooms with truth, so that in our hour of need we can bring forth both the old and the new as a source of rich provision. I pray that this study would be for you a source of much treasure and that you would labor well to obtain it.

Grace and peace,

Jen Wilkin

HOW TO USE THIS STUDY

This workbook is designed to be used in a specific way. The homework in the workbook will start you in the process of comprehension, interpretation, and application. However, it was designed to dovetail with small-group discussion time and the video teaching sessions. You can use the workbook by itself, but you are likely to find yourself with some unresolved questions. The video teaching sessions are intended to resolve most, if not all, of your unanswered questions from the homework and discussion time. You'll find detailed information for how to access the video teaching sessions that accompany this study in the back of your workbook. With this in mind, consider using the materials as follows:

You'll find detailed information for how to **ACCESS THE VIDEO TEACHING SESSIONS** that accompany this study in the back of your workbook.

- If you are going through the study **on your own**, first work through the homework, and then watch the corresponding video teaching for that week.

- If you are going through the study **in a group**, first do your homework, and then discuss the questions your group decides to cover. Then watch the video teaching. Some groups watch the teaching before they meet, which can also work if that format fits best for everyone. Group leaders, you'll find promotional materials and more tools to help you lead at **lifeway.com/sermononthemount**.

Note: For Week One, there is no homework. The study begins with a video introduction. You will find a Viewer Guide on pages 18–19 that you can use as you watch the introductory material.

HOW TO USE THE GROUP DISCUSSION GUIDE

At the end of each week's homework you will find a leader guide intended to help facilitate discussion in small groups. The group discussion guide includes questions to help group members compare what they have learned from their homework. These questions are either pulled directly from the homework, or they summarize a concept or theme that the homework covered. Each section covers content from a particular day of the homework, first asking group members to reflect on their observations and then asking them to apply. The observation questions typically ask group members to report a finding or flesh out an interpretation. The application questions challenge them to move beyond intellectual understanding and to identify ways to live differently in light of what they have learned.

As a small group leader, you will want to review these questions before you meet with your group, thinking through your own answers, marking where they occur in the homework, and noting if there are any additional questions you might want to reference to help the flow of the discussion. These questions are suggestions only, intended to help you cover as much ground as you can in a forty-five-minute discussion time. They should not be seen as requirements or limitations, but as guidelines to help you prepare your group for the teaching time by allowing them to process collectively what they have learned during their homework.

As a facilitator of discussion rather than a teacher, you are allowed and encouraged to be a colearner with your group members. This means you yourself may not always feel confident of your answer to a given question, and that is perfectly OK. Because we are studying for the long-term, we are allowed to leave some questions partially answered or unresolved, trusting for clarity at a later time. In most cases, the video teaching time should address any lingering questions that are not resolved in the homework or the small-group discussion time.

week one

THE KINGDOM
OF HEAVEN

Seeing the crowds, he went
up on the mountain,
and when he sat down, his
disciples came to him.

MATTHEW 5:1

The Kingdom of Heaven

Watch the teaching video for Week One. Use the space provided to take notes.

MATTHEW 5:1

Seeing the crowds, he went up on the mountain,

and when he sat down, his disciples came to him.

Why are there _____ **?**

Who is Jesus's _____ **for the Sermon on the Mount?**

    Primary:

    Secondary:

Why does Jesus _____ **?**

Psalm 80:1-2	Throne
Psalm 99:1	Throne
Hebrews 1:3	Right hand of Majesty

To access the video teaching sessions, use the instructions in the back of your workbook.

Why is Jesus _____ ?

1.	**Matthew 4:8**	Temptation
2.	**Matthew 5:1**	Sermon on the Mount
3.	**Matthew 14:23**	Goes up alone to pray all night
4.	**Matthew 15:29**	Heals the crowds; feeding of four thousand
5.	**Matthew 17:1-8**	Transfiguration
6.	**Matthew 24:3**	Olivet Discourse
7.	**Matthew 28:16-20**	Great Commission

Before you begin your Week Two homework, be sure to read the Foreword (pp. 8–12) for an explanation of the Bible study method used in this study.

week two

WHO IS BLESSED?

Each week you will start your homework by reading through the entire Sermon on the Mount from start to finish. Then you'll focus in on a particular passage to discover its message and how it fits into the greater context of the sermon as a whole. By the time you complete this study, you will have read the Sermon on the Mount at least nine times. As it grows more familiar to you, watch for how your understanding deepens and expands. Your first task each week will be to note how this process is taking place. To help you read for detail, you'll be asked to mark certain words or phrases in the copy of Matthew 5–7 printed on pages 176–187 of this book. Keep a set of colored pencils or markers handy as you read.

This week we'll focus our study efforts on dissecting the eight short statements that form the opening to Jesus's longest recorded message—statements commonly known as the Beatitudes. You may be familiar with some or all of them. We'll strive to look at them with fresh eyes, asking ourselves why, of all the ways Jesus could have begun His inaugural address to His disciples, He began with a list of "blesseds."

DAY ONE

READ MATTHEW 5:1–7:29 ON PAGES 176–187.

As you read, ⟨circle⟩ each occurrence of the word *righteousness* with a blue pencil or marker. We will be considering its meaning and use on Day Three.

1. Which section of the sermon seems unclear to you?

2. Which section seems most straightforward?

3. Look up the word *beatitude* in the dictionary or thesaurus. Write the definition below.

    Beatitude:

4. Why do you think Jesus chooses to begin the Sermon on the Mount with a list of "blesseds"?

DAY TWO

² And he opened his mouth and taught them, saying:

³ Blessed are the poor in spirit, for theirs is the kingdom of heaven.

⁴ Blessed are those who mourn, for they shall be comforted.

MATTHEW 5:2-4

5. Look up the following passages, and note what each teaches us about being poor.

   Psalm 40:16-17:

   Psalm 69:32-33:

   Psalm 72:12-14:

   Isaiah 66:2 (*humble* is translated "poor" in the KJV):

   What kind of poverty is addressed in these verses?

6. Webster's Dictionary defines *poverty* as "the state of one with insufficient resources."[1] Based on this definition, what does it mean to be "poor in spirit"?

---

1. Merriam-Webster's Collegiate Dictionary, s.v. "poverty," accessed June 20, 2023, https://unabridged. merriam-webster.com/collegiate/poverty.

7. What does Jesus say belongs to those who are poor in spirit?

In our video introduction in Week One, we defined the *kingdom of heaven* as "the kingdom of grace here, and the kingdom of glory hereafter." It's the reign of God established at Christ's first coming and consummated (completed) at His second coming. It's the rule of God particularly over believers.

8. Why do you think Jesus says that the kingdom of heaven belongs to the "poor in spirit"?

9. Now look at the second Beatitude in Matthew 5:4. People can mourn for many reasons. What are some things that cause us to mourn?

COMPARE JOEL 2:12-13 AND JAMES 4:7-10.

10. What do we learn about the role of mourning in these passages?

11. In light of these passages and in light of the first Beatitude, what kind of mourning do you think Jesus is referring to when He says, "Blessed are those who mourn"?

12. **APPLY:** How has recognizing your lack of spiritual resources been a blessing to you? What role has godly grief played in your repentance?

Give an example of a time each of these two blessings has operated in your life.

13. Rewrite (paraphrase) the first and second Beatitudes in your own words, getting as close to their intended meaning as you can.

DAY THREE

5 Blessed are the meek, for they shall inherit the earth.

6 Blessed are those who hunger and thirst for righteousness, for they shall be satisfied.

MATTHEW 5:5-6

Webster's Dictionary defines *meek* as "enduring injury with patience and without resentment."[2] A meek person is someone who is not occupied with self at all, someone who does not insist on a set of rights.

14. **READ ISAIAH 53.** Based on this prophetic passage and on Webster's definition of the word *meek*, how did Christ perfectly demonstrate meekness?

15. How would having a true estimate of ourselves in relation to God help us be meek?

16. What would the world say is a synonym for *meek*?

---

2. Merriam-Webster's Collegiate Dictionary, s.v. "meek," accessed June 20, 2023, https://unabridged. merriam-webster.com/collegiate/meek.

17. How does the third Beatitude contrast with the world's opinion of who will "inherit the earth"?

18. In what sense do you think the meek will inherit the earth?

19. **APPLY**: If a meek person is someone who does not insist on a set of rights, how meek are you? What rights do you feel entitled to or take for granted in your home, church, workplace, or community?

How can a sense of entitlement stifle your relationship with God or skew your perception of God?

20. Now look at the fourth Beatitude in Matthew 5:6. On Day One you circled the word *righteousness* with a blue pencil or marker. How many times does it occur in the sermon?

21. Look up the word righteousness in the dictionary or thesaurus. Write the definition below.

Righteousness:

22. Look up the following passages and answer the questions for each.

JOHN 4:7-10:

Who is speaking in verse 10? _____

What is offered? _____

What need is satisfied? _____

JOHN 6:35:

Who is speaking? _____

What is offered? _____

What need is satisfied? _____

23. **READ 1 CORINTHIANS 1:26-31.** According to verse 30, who is our righteousness?

24. **APPLY:** We hunger and thirst after many things besides righteousness. What are you hungering and thirsting for right now that cannot satisfy? List your thoughts below.

25. In what ways are these things poor substitutes for Christ?

26. Rewrite (paraphrase) the third and fourth Beatitudes in your own words, getting as close to their intended meaning as you can.

DAY FOUR

⁷ Blessed are the merciful, for they shall receive mercy.

⁸ Blessed are the pure in heart, for they shall see God.

MATTHEW 5:7-8

27. How would you define *mercy*? How does justice relate to mercy? Use a dictionary or thesaurus to help with your answer.

28. **READ MATTHEW 7:1-2.** What concept is presented in this later passage of the Sermon on the Mount that is also presented in the fifth Beatitude?

29. Why do you think how we treat others will affect how God treats us?

30. **APPLY:** To whom do you have difficulty showing mercy? How could you adjust your perspective so that showing mercy to that person becomes easier?

31. **NOW LOOK AT THE SIXTH BEATITUDE, MATTHEW 5:8.** Think about what Jesus means by "pure in heart." How would you respond to someone who defined "pure in heart" as sinless? Look up 1 John 1:8 to help with your answer.

32. If being pure in heart is not being perfect or free from sin, what is it?

33. Why do you think the pure in heart will "see God"?

34. **READ ISAIAH 6:1-8.** Was Isaiah "pure in heart"? Why or why not?

35. **APPLY:** In what specific areas of your life do you battle impurity of heart?

How do these areas of sin cloud your ability to "see God"?

36. Rewrite (paraphrase) the fifth and sixth Beatitudes in your own words, getting as close to their intended meaning as you can.

DAY FIVE

⁹ Blessed are the peacemakers, for they shall be called sons of God.

¹⁰ Blessed are those who are persecuted for righteousness' sake, for theirs is the kingdom of heaven.

¹¹ Blessed are you when others revile you and persecute you and utter all kinds of evil against you falsely on my account.

¹² Rejoice and be glad, for your reward is great in heaven, for so they persecuted the prophets who were before you.

MATTHEW 5:9-12

37. Look up the word *peacemaker* in a dictionary or thesaurus, and write the definition below. Note any synonyms you think would fit with the way Jesus uses the word *peacemaker* in the seventh Beatitude.

Peacemaker:

38. **READ ISAIAH 9:6.** Which of the titles given for Jesus relates to the seventh Beatitude?

39. **READ GALATIANS 4:4-7.** Based on these verses and your answer to the previous question, why do you think the peacemakers will be called the "sons of God"?

40. **APPLY:** What are practical ways to be a practicing peacemaker? Think of specific ways you can use your speech and actions to be a peacemaker, and note them below.

In your home:

In your church:

In your community/workplace:

In your country:

41. What is the contrast between the seventh and eighth Beatitudes? In other words, why would a peacemaker ever be the object of persecution?

42. For what reason does the eighth Beatitude say persecution will occur?

"for _____ _____ "

43. Look back at Day Three, question 23. Who did we learn is our righteousness (see 1 Cor. 1:30)?

How does Matthew 5:11 confirm this connection?

44. In Matthew 5:11-12, Jesus restates and expands upon the eighth Beatitude. Why does He say persecution is reason for rejoicing?

45. **APPLY:** Have you ever been persecuted "for righteousness' sake"? Think about how the experience changed you. Did you feel "blessed"? Share your thoughts below.

46. Rewrite (paraphrase) the seventh and eighth Beatitudes in your own words, getting as close to their intended meaning as you can.

WRAP-UP

What impacted you most in this week's passage from the Sermon on the Mount? How has Jesus challenged your concept of what it means to be "blessed"?

Introductory Question: Describe your most memorable encounter with someone who is famous. How did you respond and why?

1. Reflect: Based on your Day Two study this week, why should we desire to be poor in spirit and mourn?

Apply: (question 12, p. 25) How has recognizing your lack of spiritual resources been a blessing to you? What role has godly grief played in your repentance? Give an example of a time each of these two blessings has operated in your life.

2. Reflect: (question 14, p. 26) Based on Isaiah 53, how did Christ perfectly demonstrate meekness?

Apply: (question 19, p. 27) If a meek person is someone who does not insist on a set of rights, how meek are you? What rights do you feel entitled to or take for granted in your home, church, workplace, or community? How can a sense of entitlement stifle your relationship with God or skew your perception of God?

3. Reflect: On Day Four we learned about being merciful and pure in heart. How are these two blessed qualities related to each other? Can we be one without being the other?

Apply: (question 30, p. 30) To whom do you have difficulty showing mercy? How could you adjust your perspective so that showing mercy to that person becomes easier?

4. Reflect: What is a peacemaker? How was Jesus a peacemaker?

Apply: (question 40, p. 34) What are practical ways to be a practicing peacemaker in your home, church, community/workplace, or country?

5. Wrap-up: (p. 35) What impacted you most in this week's passage from the Sermon on the Mount? How has Jesus challenged your concept of what it means to be "blessed"?

Who Is Blessed?

Watch the teaching video for Week Two. Use the space provided to take notes.

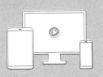

To access the video teaching sessions, use the instructions in the back of your workbook.

After the video concludes, close your study in prayer. Praise God for blessing those the world calls cursed. Ask God to help you walk toward Him in humility, meekness, repentance, and hunger for truth. Ask Him to help you walk toward others in mercy, purity, peace, and righteousness. Thank Him that He sent Jesus to become a curse for us, that we might be called blessed.

week three

A PEOPLE OF INFLUENCE

Last week we learned whom Jesus considered blessed. We listened as He turned His disciples' expectations for what it meant to be a citizen of the kingdom of heaven upside down; rather than kings and conquerors, citizens of the kingdom should expect to be aliens and strangers. Rather than pursue a political agenda, citizens should expect to pursue a spiritual one. Rather than a kingdom established through the conquest of its rulers, citizens should expect a kingdom established through the character of its servants.

In eight simple statements, Jesus explained to His listeners where this character takes root and how it bears fruit. Character, He said, takes root in spiritual poverty, grief, submission, and famine (see Matt. 5:3-6). Character, He said, bears the fruit of compassion, purification, reconciliation, and identification (see Matt. 5:7-10). When we answer the call to discipleship, we enter into a kingdom that turns human expectations of blessedness upside down.

Having illuminated the character of the citizens of the kingdom of heaven, Jesus will now move on to examine their influence on the world around them. He does so with two simple illustrations drawn from everyday life: salt and light. And He issues a call to righteousness that will boggle the minds of those gathered to hear Him teach.

DAY ONE

READ MATTHEW 5:1–7:29 ON PAGES 176–187.

Circle each occurrence of the phrase "kingdom of heaven" with a red pencil or marker.

1. How many times does this phrase occur?

2. Has your understanding of a difficult passage improved with repeated reading this week? In what ways?

   Has a straightforward passage taken on deeper meaning for you with repeated reading this week? In what ways?

3. In Matthew 5:1-12, what is Jesus's main point? Summarize this section in a phrase or sentence.

4. In Matthew 5:13-16, what is Jesus's main point? Summarize this section in a phrase or sentence.

5. In Matthew 5:17-19, what is Jesus's main point? Summarize this section in a phrase or sentence.

DAY TWO

You are the salt of the earth, but if salt has lost its taste, how shall its saltiness be restored? It is no longer good for anything except to be thrown out and trampled under people's feet.

MATTHEW 5:13

Before refrigeration, salt was used as a preservative to keep meat from rotting. In the following passages, salt is mentioned for a specific reason. Read each passage, and note what you learn about salt.

READ GENESIS 19:1-26.

6. What role does salt play in this passage?

7. Why do you think Lot's wife was turned into a pillar of salt (v. 26)?

8. Why do you think salt is specifically mentioned, rather than some other substance?

READ LEVITICUS 2:11-13.

9. What role does salt play in this passage?

10. Why do you think salt is specifically mentioned, rather than some other substance?

COMPARE NUMBERS 18:19 AND 2 CHRONICLES 13:5.

11. What common "salty" phrase do they share?

12. Why do you think God would combine the ideas of covenant and salt?

13. What does Jesus mean when He refers to His disciples as the "salt of the earth"?

14. **APPLY:** What are some specific ways believers can be "salt" in this world?

What relationship in your life needs salt?

DAY THREE

[14] You are the light of the world. A city set on a hill cannot be hidden. [15] Nor do people light a lamp and put it under a basket, but on a stand, and it gives light to all in the house. [16] In the same way, let your light shine before others, so that they may see your good works and give glory to your Father who is in heaven.

MATTHEW 5:14-16

15. What are some of the functions of light in the natural world?

16. How does the analogy of "light" illustrate the role of Jesus's disciples in the world?

17. When our light shines before men, what is it that will be noticeable about us? (Check one.)

    ☐   Our prosperous lifestyle

    ☐   The words we speak

    ☐   The good we do

    Why do you think this is so?

18. **READ 1 JOHN 1:5-7; 2:7-11.** Record each phrase containing *darkness* or *light* under the appropriate heading in the chart below.

DARKNESS	LIGHT

19. In what sense is the church a light to the world?

20. How does the church's role as light *differ* from its role as salt?

21. How does the church's role as light *complement* its role as salt?

22. According to Matthew 5:16, how will those around us respond as we shine forth the light of truth?

23. **APPLY:** Is there a specific situation in which God is calling you to be the light of truth? What holds you back from fulfilling your role as the light of the world?

24. Restate the following in your own words.

"You are the salt of the earth."

"You are the light of the world."

DAY FOUR

17 Do not think that I have come to abolish the Law or the Prophets; I have not come to abolish them but to fulfill them. 18 For truly, I say to you, until heaven and earth pass away, not an iota, not a dot, will pass from the Law until all is accomplished.

MATTHEW 5:17-18

25. In Matthew 5:17, Jesus addresses the silent conclusion of His disciples, based on what He told them in Matthew 5:1-16. In other words, verses 1-16 would lead the disciples to think, *Jesus means to do away with the Law and the Prophets!* Why would the disciples come to this conclusion?

NOW READ MATTHEW 5:17-20.

26. How do Jesus's comments in Matthew 5:17-20 set up His listeners for what will follow in Matthew 5:21–6:18?

27. What was the role of a prophet in the Old Testament? (Look up the term *prophet* in a dictionary or thesaurus if you need a little help.) Check one answer below.

      ☐   to offer the sacrifices in the temple

      ☐   to give his interpretation of the will of God

      ☐   to serve as a mouthpiece for the words of God

28. What do you think Jesus means when He speaks of "the Law and the Prophets"? What is He referring to?

29. Scripture teaches that the Law is given for a threefold purpose: to reveal sin, to establish decency in society, and to provide a rule of life. Match the following verses with the use of the Law they demonstrate.

Exodus 20:12-17   The Law reveals sin.

Romans 13:8-10   The Law provides a rule of life.

Romans 3:19-20   The Law establishes decency in society.

30. Webster defines fulfill as "to make full; to measure up to; to satisfy."[1] In what way(s) do you think Christ fulfills each of these three aspects of the Law? **READ JOHN 8:1-11**, and note below how Jesus fulfills each aspect of the law in the story related there.

THE LAW	CHRIST FULFILLS THE LAW
Reveals Sin	
Establishes decency in society	
Provides a rule of life	

The Law given in the Old Testament can be understood in three categories: moral law, like the Ten Commandments, civil law, like the laws governing restitution in Exodus 22, and ceremonial law, like the regulations found in the book of Leviticus.

Old Testament ceremonial law was given as part of the Mosaic covenant at Mount Sinai. It dictated the rules and regulations for ritual cleanliness that allowed a person to commune with a holy God. Second, it dictated regulations regarding everyday life—food, work on the Sabbath, whom one could marry—which served to distinguish the Jews from their Gentile neighbors as the chosen people of God. Civil law was given so that Israel's judges could maintain justice in the community of God's people. It was specific to a particular historical context. Moral law underpinned both ceremonial and civil law, transcending any particular era in history. The Pharisees were experts in observing outwardly the ceremonial, civil, and moral law.

---

1. Merriam-Webster's Collegiate Dictionary, s.v. "fulfill," accessed June 20, 2023, https://unabridged.merriam-webster.com/collegiate/fulfill.

31. **READ ACTS 10:9-16; 11:1-18.** What do Peter and the other apostles conclude from Peter's vision?

32. **READ MARK 7:14-16.** How do Jesus's words shed further light on the issue of clean and unclean things?

33. **APPLY:** If "not the smallest letter, not the least stroke of a pen, will by any means disappear from the Law until everything is accomplished" (Matt. 5:18, NIV), why do we no longer observe ceremonial law? Why do we no longer sacrifice animals, cleanse ourselves before worshiping, or avoid certain foods?

DAY FIVE

¹⁹ Therefore whoever relaxes one of the least of these commandments and teaches others to do the same will be called least in the kingdom of heaven, but whoever does them and teaches them will be called great in the kingdom of heaven. ²⁰ For I tell you, unless your righteousness exceeds that of the scribes and Pharisees, you will never enter the kingdom of heaven.

MATTHEW 5:19-20

34. How are we guilty of relaxing the commands of God? Give a general statement of how we do this, followed by a specific example.

35. Why do you think Jesus says those who relax God's commands and teach others to do the same will be called "least in the kingdom of heaven"?

36. In Matthew 5:19, Jesus states, "whoever *practices and teaches* these commands will be called great in the kingdom of heaven" (NIV, emphasis mine). What is the implied relationship between practicing and teaching the commands of God?

37. Who were the scribes and the Pharisees? Look up each term in the dictionary or thesaurus, and write a definition for each that fits the historical context of this passage.

> **Scribe:** *(compare the NIV of Matthew 5:20 to help with your definition)*

> **Pharisee:**

Based on your definitions, do you think the scribes and Pharisees were highly regarded or lowly regarded within society?

38. In Week Two, we defined *righteousness* as utter purity of character. What sort of righteousness did the scribes and Pharisees possess? Read Matthew 23:1-7 to check your answer.

In light of your answer above, what sort of righteousness could ever exceed that of the Pharisees?

39. **APPLY:** The Great Commission tells us all believers are called to teach the commands of God to others. Who has God placed in your life to teach? How can your actions better align with the commands you are teaching?

Pray and ask God to help you teach only that which you practice and practice only that which you teach.

WRAP-UP

What impacted you most in this week's passage from the Sermon on the Mount? What are the words of Jesus asking of you personally?

WEEK THREE | GROUP DISCUSSION

INTRODUCTORY QUESTION: Describe your biggest cooking catastrophe.

1. REFLECT: In the introduction to the Day Two homework, you read that salt was primarily used as a preservative before refrigeration. Look back over the questions from Day Two. What do you think salt symbolizes in these passages?

APPLY: (question 14, p. 45) What are some specific ways believers can be "salt" in this world? What relationship in your life needs salt?

2. REFLECT: (questions 15–16, p. 46) What are some of the functions of light in the natural world? How does the analogy of "light" illustrate the role of Jesus's disciples in the world?

APPLY: (question 23, p. 48) Is there a specific situation in which God is calling you to be the light of truth? What holds you back from fulfilling your role as the light of the world?

3. REFLECT: (question 25, p. 49) In Matthew 5:17, Jesus addresses the silent conclusion of His disciples, based on what He told them in Matthew 5:1-16. In other words, verses 1-16 would lead the disciples to think, *Jesus means to do away with the Law and the Prophets!* Why would the disciples come to this conclusion?

APPLY: (question 33, p. 52) If "not the smallest letter, not the least stroke of a pen, will by any means disappear from the Law until everything is accomplished" (Matt. 5:18, NIV), why do we no longer observe ceremonial law? Why do we no longer sacrifice animals, cleanse ourselves before worshiping, or avoid certain foods?

4. REFLECT: (question 38, p. 54) What sort of righteousness could ever exceed that of the Pharisees?

APPLY: (question 39, p. 55) The Great Commission tells us all believers are called to teach the commands of God to others. Who has God placed in your life to teach? How can your actions better align with the commands you are teaching?

5. WRAP-UP: (p. 55) What impacted you most in this week's passage from the Sermon on the Mount? What are the words of Jesus asking of you personally?

A People of Influence

Watch the teaching video for Week Three. Use the space provided to take notes.

To access the video teaching sessions, use the instructions in the back of your workbook.

After the video concludes, close your study in prayer. Praise God for sending Christ to fulfill all righteousness on our behalf. Ask Him to show you where you have trusted in your own righteousness. Ask Him for the courage to be salt and light in your key relationships. Thank God that through the finished work of Christ, we have been given a righteousness that renders us fit for heaven.

week four

"YOU HAVE HEARD
THAT IT WAS SAID ..."

PART 1

Last week we learned that those who follow Christ are people of influence. As spiritual salt, we prevent moral decay. And as spiritual light, we promote the growth of righteousness. We learned that Jesus did not come to do away with the Law, but to fulfill it through a deeper obedience. And we marveled with Jesus's original hearers that God required a greater righteousness than that demonstrated by the most religious people we know.

This week we will discover what Jesus means by a "righteousness [that] exceeds that of the scribes and Pharisees" (Matt. 5:20). Jesus will turn our attention to the Law itself, exploring the distance between the hypocrisy of those whose outward obedience to the Law of God conceals a heart that is far from the God of the Law. Of all of the Ten Commandments, the commands against committing murder and adultery can seem to us like the easiest to avoid. No doubt, Jesus's listeners thought the same. So it's there that Jesus will begin His examination of the nature of true righteousness, with the intent not to condemn us, but to set us free.

DAY ONE

READ MATTHEW 5:1–7:29 ON PAGES 176–187.

As you read, <u>underline</u> every occurrence of the phrases "you have heard that it was said" and "it was also said" with an orange pencil or marker.

1. To whom do you think Jesus is referring with this phrase? Who "said" what had been heard? Check one.

    ☐   God

    ☐   the prophets

    ☐   the teachers of the Law

Now <u>underline</u> every occurrence of the phrases "But I say to you," "Truly, I say to you," and "I tell you" with a purple pencil or marker.

2. Why do you think Jesus uses these phrases repeatedly?

3. Why might they cause offense to His hearers?

DAY TWO

You have heard that it was said to those of old, "You shall not murder; and whoever murders will be liable to judgment."

MATTHEW 5:21

READ EXODUS 20:13. COMPARE IT TO MATTHEW 5:21-26.

4. According to Matthew 5:21, what had the people heard? Had they been taught wrongly?

5. How does Jesus respond? Does He contradict what they had heard?

6. Matthew 5:22 gives three more things for which people would be held accountable. List them below.

7. **READ EPHESIANS 4:26.** Do you think it is a sin to be angry? What is the difference between sinful anger and "unsinful" anger?

Give an example of each.

Sinful anger:

Unsinful anger:

8. Can you think of a story in Scripture that would prove whether or not it is always a sin to be angry? Share it here.

9. **REREAD MATTHEW 5:21-22 IN THE NIV.** *Raca* is the Aramaic word for empty-headed or stupid. The word *fool* means morally worthless. Both are expressions of contempt, but *fool* is assigned greater punishment than *raca*. Why do you think this is the case?

10. Look up the terms *anger* and *contempt* in your dictionary or thesaurus. Write a brief definition for each.

Anger:

Contempt:

11. What is the difference between these two emotions? How are they related?

12. What relationship between anger, contempt, and murder do you think Jesus is pointing out in this passage?

13. **APPLY:** Jesus specifically links anger to sinful speech. How has your own anger resulted in sinful speech? List specific forms of speech your anger has taken.

Pray and ask God to help you deal with your anger before your words can harmfully express it.

DAY THREE

²³ So if you are offering your gift at the altar and there remember that your brother has something against you, ²⁴ leave your gift there before the altar and go. First be reconciled to your brother, and then come and offer your gift. ²⁵ Come to terms quickly with your accuser while you are going with him to court, lest your accuser hand you over to the judge, and the judge to the guard, and you be put in prison. ²⁶ Truly, I say to you, you will never get out until you have paid the last penny.

MATTHEW 5:23-26

14. In Matthew 5:23-26, what does Jesus want to teach us about fractured relationships?

15. When we offend someone, why is it important to go to that person and deal with the offense immediately?

16. How does unreconciled anger affect our ability to worship God (see Matt. 5:24)?

17. Think of someone toward whom you harbor anger or contempt. Consider how your anger has affected your relationship with that person.

How has it affected the other person?

How has it affected you?

What sinful actions have resulted from your anger?

18. **APPLY:** Why do you think we tend to hold onto our anger rather than letting it go?

What should we do if the person with whom we want to reconcile has no desire to do so? What if the person we need to reconcile with is no longer living?

19. Pray and ask God to show you how to reconcile the relationship you've been reflecting on. Write down any ideas that come to mind.

DAY FOUR

You have heard that it was said, "You shall not commit adultery."

MATTHEW 5:27

READ EXODUS 20:14 AND MATTHEW 5:27-30.

20. According to Matthew 5:27, what had the people heard? Had they been taught wrongly?

21. How does Jesus respond? Does He contradict what they had heard?

22. Is Jesus's discussion of anger and contempt in any way related to His discussion of adultery? Explain your answer.

23. In Matthew 5:29-30, does Jesus set forth a course of action to be followed literally? Why or why not? What point do you think He wants to make?

24. Match the following reference to its main thought.

Mark 8:34	Put to death the misdeeds of the body
Romans 8:12-14	Put to death immorality, impurity, passion, evil desire, covetousness
Galatians 5:24-25	Deny yourself and take up your cross
Colossians 3:1-5	Crucify the sinful nature's passions and desires

25. What light do these verses shed on Jesus's words about tearing out eyes and cutting off hands?

26. **APPLY:** What are some examples of ways you can crucify the flesh daily? In other words, in what areas of your life do you need to figuratively tear out an eye or cut off a hand?

DAY FIVE

You have heard that it was said, "You shall not commit adultery."

MATTHEW 5:27

READ JOB 31:1-12 IN THE NIV.

27. What type of covenant did Job make?

"I have made a covenant _____ _____ _____ not to

_____ _____ at a _____ _____."

(Job 31:1, NIV)

28. List below the "ifs" and "thens" of Job's statement.

IF	THEN

How seriously did Job take the issue of adultery?

29. Why do you think adultery is not taken seriously?

30. On the issues of murder and adultery, how does Jesus challenge a casual view of what it means to be righteous? Paraphrase His views on the two topics.

Murder:

Adultery:

31. **APPLY:** Have you been casual in your approach to the sins of murder and adultery? How can you take them more seriously? Write some specific thoughts.

WRAP-UP

What impacted you most in this week's passage from the Sermon on the Mount? What are the words of Jesus on dealing with anger, murder, and adultery asking of you personally?

WEEK FOUR | GROUP DISCUSSION

INTRODUCTORY QUESTION: What is the best part of your weekend?

1. REFLECT: (question 7, p. 64) Do you think it is a sin to be angry? What is the difference between sinful anger and "unsinful" anger?

APPLY: (question 13, p. 65) Jesus specifically links anger to sinful speech. How has your own anger resulted in sinful speech? List specific forms of speech your anger has taken.

2. REFLECT: (question 14, p. 66) In Matthew 5:23-26, what does Jesus want to teach us about fractured relationships?

APPLY: (question 18, p. 68) Why do you think we tend to hold onto our anger rather than letting it go? What should we do if the person with whom we want to reconcile has no desire to do so? What if the person we need to reconcile with is no longer living?

3. REFLECT: (question 23, p. 69) In Matthew 5:29-30, does Jesus set forth a course of action to be followed literally? Why or why not? What point do you think He wants to make?

APPLY: (question 26, p. 70) What are some examples of ways you can crucify the flesh daily? In other words, in what areas of your life do you need to figuratively tear out an eye or cut off a hand?

4. **REFLECT:** (question 30, p. 72) On the issues of murder and adultery, how does Jesus challenge a casual view of what it means to be righteous?

APPLY: (question 31, p. 73) Have you been casual in your approach to the sins of murder and adultery? How can you take them more seriously?

5. **WRAP-UP:** (p. 73) What impacted you most in this week's passage from the Sermon on the Mount? What are the words of Jesus on dealing with anger, murder, and adultery asking of you personally?

"You Have Heard That It Was Said . . ." Part 1

Watch the teaching video for Week Four. Use the space provided to take notes.

To access the video teaching sessions, use the instructions in the back of your workbook.

After the video concludes, close your study in prayer. Ask God to show you where you have wanted to "walk the line" rather than flee from sin with regard to anger and lust. Ask Him to teach you to deal ruthlessly with sin. Praise Him that because of the cross He is no longer angry with us. Thank Him for His faithfulness to you and for His forgiveness of all your sins of the past, present, and future.

week five

"YOU HAVE HEARD THAT IT WAS SAID ..."

PART 2

Last week Jesus began answering the question, "What does the righteousness of a follower of Christ look like?" He challenged us to a deeper obedience to the Law, one in which both our actions and our motives are pure. We considered the difference between asking, "How far is too far?" and asking, "How can I flee from sin?"

Having examined the root sins behind murder and adultery, Jesus now turns His attention to three further areas of the Law that had been taught in harmful ways: divorce, oaths, and restitution. Much of what He has to say is hard to hear, particularly to our modern ears. This particular section of the Sermon on the Mount has been the source of much controversy. Is a divorced woman who remarries an adulteress? Is it a sin to swear an oath in a court of law or to say the Pledge of Allegiance? Should we allow our enemies to take advantage of us to our harm? It would seem that we, too, "have heard that it was said."

I can't think of a better reason to look closely at these verses in context to see what Jesus would have us learn. Perhaps His original hearers were not the only ones who needed clarification on the true nature of righteousness.

DAY ONE

READ MATTHEW 5:1–7:29 IN THE CSB TRANSLATION.

1. Next to each section of the sermon we have studied thus far, write a phrase that summarizes its message.

    Matthew 5:1-12:

    Matthew 5:13-16:

    Matthew 5:17-20:

    Matthew 5:21-26:

    Matthew 5:27-30:

    Now transfer your summary statements to the margin of your copy of the text on pages 176–187, writing them next to the section they summarize.

2. How does what Jesus talked about in Matthew 5:21-30 flow logically into His discussion in Matthew 5:31-48?

DAY TWO

It was also said, "Whoever divorces his wife, let him give her a certificate of divorce."

MATTHEW 5:31

Divorce is a painful and personal topic for many of us. It's also a difficult topic to study in Scripture. As you read today, pray and ask God to help you set aside the lens of your own experience or of past teaching you have heard. Ask Him to help you read carefully for the original meaning and intent of the passages we will study. Ask Him to remind you of His infinite goodness in all He commands.

READ DEUTERONOMY 24:1-4 AND MATTHEW 5:31-32.

3. According to Matthew 5:31, what had the people heard? Had they been taught wrongly?

4. How does Jesus respond? Does He contradict what they had heard? Explain your answer.

NOW READ MATTHEW 19:3-9. Jesus spoke further here on the topic of marriage and remarriage.

5. The Pharisees wanted to test Jesus with a question about divorce. How does Jesus's reply in Matthew 19:4-6 contrast with their question?

6. How do Jesus's words in Matthew 19:3-9 shed further light on His meaning in Matthew 5:31-32? Is Jesus forbidding divorce or second marriages? (This is a tough one, so give your best answer based on the text. We'll discuss this further in the video teaching time.)

7. In Matthew 19:7-8, for what reason does Jesus say Moses allowed a man to divorce his wife?

_____ of _____

What kinds of behaviors might fall under this description?

8. **LOOK UP PSALM 11:5** and fill in the blanks:

The Lord tests the righteous,
but his soul hates the wicked and the one who _____ _____.

NOW READ EPHESIANS 5:25-32.
How will Christ present His bride's spiritual body?

"without _____ or _____ or any such thing, that

she might be holy and without _____ " (v. 27)

How are husbands to treat their wives' physical bodies?

"as their own _____ . . . For no one ever hated his own flesh,

but _____ and _____ it, just as Christ does

the church" (vv. 28-29)

Based on your answers, what might be an example of the kind of hardness of heart for which Moses allowed divorce?

9.   How does a high view of marriage command a Christ follower to treat his/her spouse?

10. **APPLY:** If divorce has impacted your life directly, in what way are Jesus's words painful to hear?

How are His words comforting? How do they protect what is good?

DAY THREE

Again you have heard that it was said to those of old, "You shall not swear falsely, but shall perform to the Lord what you have sworn."

MATTHEW 5:33

11. Read the following passages and note what you learn about oath-taking in the Old Testament.

Exodus 20:7:

Leviticus 19:11-12:

Numbers 30:1-2:

Deuteronomy 23:21-23:

READ MATTHEW 5:33-37.

12. According to verse 33, what had the people heard? Had they been taught wrongly?

13. How does Jesus respond? Does He contradict what they had heard? Explain.

14. Some people have taken Jesus's words to mean that a Christian should never take an oath of any kind (Pledge of Allegiance, oath of office, etc.). How would you respond to this interpretation?

15. Restate in your own words what you think Jesus means by, "Let what you say be simply 'Yes' or 'No'; anything more than this comes from evil" (Matt. 5:37).

16. How has our culture relaxed this teaching?

17. **APPLY:** Have you ever verbally committed to do something you later failed to do? Think of a time when you have broken your word. Why do you think it is particularly important for Christ followers to be as good as their word?

    What steps can you take to align your words with your commitments? How can you begin to stop over-promising and/or under-delivering?

DAY FOUR

You have heard that it was said, "An eye for an eye and a tooth for a tooth."

MATTHEW 5:38

READ LEVITICUS 24:20 AND MATTHEW 5:38-42.

18. According to Matthew 5:38, what had the people heard? Had they been taught wrongly?

19. How does Jesus respond? Does He contradict what they had heard? Explain your thoughts.

CAREFULLY READ DEUTERONOMY 19:16-21.

20. Based on the context, to whom was the instruction "an eye for an eye" given (19:21)? Check one:

☐ the accuser

☐ the accused

☐ the judges

21. Based on your answer to the previous question, how do you think the teachers of the Law were wrongly applying the principle of "an eye for an eye"?

22. What do you think was the positive intent of this law as given in the Old Testament? How could it protect the accused as well as the accuser?

23. Which of the Beatitudes seems to fit best with Jesus's description of responding to mistreatment (Matt. 5:39-42)? Explain your answer.

24. Why do you think believers struggle to follow the instruction Jesus gives about turning the other cheek or going the extra mile?

25. What is accomplished by turning the other cheek? What is risked?

26. Why do you think believers struggle to follow Jesus's instruction to "Give to the one who begs from you, and do not refuse the one who would borrow from you" (5:42)?

27. What types of wrong thinking prevent us from being faithful to carry out these instructions?

28. **APPLY:** Is there someone toward whom you are afraid or unwilling to practice non-retaliation? How would Jesus instruct you to respond to that person's insults or persecution?

Is there someone toward whom you are reluctant to practice giving or lending? How would Jesus instruct you to loosen your grip on your stuff?

DAY FIVE

You have heard that it was said, "You shall love your neighbor and hate your enemy."

MATTHEW 5:43

READ LEVITICUS 19:18 AND MATTHEW 5:43-48.

29. According to Matthew 5:43, what had the people heard? Had they been taught wrongly? (Be careful!)

30. How does Jesus respond? Does He contradict what they had heard? Explain your thoughts.

31. Summarize what Jesus is saying in Matthew 5:44-47.

32. What do you think it means to "be perfect, as your heavenly Father is perfect" (5:48)?

33. Look through Matthew 5:43-47 for specific "perfections" of God that are mentioned. How do they instruct us in how we should treat those around us?

34. Jesus, the Son of His Father in heaven, loved His enemies and prayed for those who persecuted Him (see Matt. 5:44-45). Did Jesus choose His enemies? In light of this, how would you define an "enemy"?

35. **APPLY:** Do you have enemies? How can you follow Christ's example in dealing with them?

36. Think back to the Beatitudes. Which character trait do you think is most necessary to fulfill the command to love those who persecute you? Why?

Ask God to help you cultivate that character trait. Ask Him to help you in specific relationships.

WRAP-UP

What impacted you most in this week's passage from the Sermon on the Mount? What are the words of Jesus on marriage, pure speech, non-retribution, and loving enemies asking of you personally?

INTRODUCTORY QUESTION: What is your favorite season of the year? Why is it your favorite?

1. REFLECT: (question 7, p. 82) In Matthew 19:7-8, for what reason does Jesus say Moses allowed a man to divorce his wife? What kinds of behaviors might fall under this description?

APPLY: How has Jesus's teaching on divorce impacted your own view of marriage?

2. REFLECT: (question 15, p. 85) Restate in your own words what you think Jesus means by, "Let what you say be simply 'Yes' or 'No'; anything more than this comes from evil" (Matt. 5:37).

APPLY: (question 17, p. 85) Have you ever verbally committed to do something you later failed to do? Think of a time when you have broken your word. Why do you think it is particularly important for Christ followers to be as good as their word? What steps can you take to align your words with your commitments? How can you begin to stop over-promising and/or under-delivering?

3. REFLECT: (question 23, p. 87) Which of the Beatitudes seems to fit best with Jesus's description of responding to mistreatment (Matt. 5:39-42)? Explain your answer.

APPLY: (question 28, p. 88) Is there someone toward whom you are afraid or unwilling to practice non-retaliation? How would Jesus instruct you to respond to that person's insults or persecution? Is there someone toward whom you are reluctant to practice giving or lending? How would Jesus instruct you to loosen your grip on your stuff?

4. **REFLECT:** (question 31, p. 89) Summarize what Jesus is saying in Matthew 5:44-47.

APPLY: (question 35, p. 90) Do you have enemies? How can you follow Christ's example in dealing with them?

5. **WRAP-UP:** (p. 91) What impacted you most in this week's passage from the Sermon on the Mount? What are the words of Jesus on marriage, pure speech, non-retribution, and loving enemies asking of you personally?

"You Have Heard That It Was Said . . . " Part 2

Watch the teaching video for Week Five. Use the space provided to take notes.

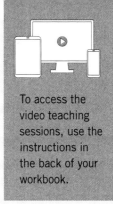

To access the video teaching sessions, use the instructions in the back of your workbook.

After the video concludes, close your study in prayer. Ask God to help you cultivate and maintain a high view of marriage. Ask Him to draw you into a deeper obedience with regard to your words and your treatment of others. Praise God that His "yes" is always "yes" and His "no" is always "no." Thank Him that He treats us not as we deserve, but with a preferential love—a love that turned its cheek and went the extra mile.

week six

SECRET
RIGHTEOUSNESS

It's probably safe to say that each of us grapples with the sin of approval seeking, of desiring to win the praise and attention of others. We even use the outwardly righteous practices of our faith to focus attention on ourselves. In Matthew 6:1-18, Jesus will address this tendency head-on.

For the past two weeks of our study, Jesus has focused on teaching a deeper obedience to the "don'ts"—don't murder, don't commit adultery, and so on. This week He begins teaching a deeper obedience to the "dos"—do give to the needy, do pray, do fast. We'll first compare these three sections of the sermon before finishing this week by studying the Lord's Prayer. Our focus will shift from considering what it truly means to do the wrong thing to what it truly means to do the right thing.

Just as we are not righteous simply by avoiding forbidden actions, we are not righteous simply by practicing commanded actions. Our motives must match our outward obedience. Jesus will continue to faithfully pry from His listeners' grip the desire to live a "bare minimum" faith—one in which we seek to invest as little effort as possible to enjoy as many benefits as possible as followers of Christ. Instead, He will point us to an abundant faith, one that breathes righteousness into even the "secret" moments of our lives.

DAY ONE

READ MATTHEW 5:1–7:29 ON PAGES 176–187.

As you read, circle each occurrence of the phrase "your [heavenly] Father" with a brown pencil or marker.

1. How many times does this phrase occur?

2. Choose a passage of the sermon that has become very familiar to you after repeated reading and study. Write it on a note card and spend some time committing it to memory.

3. Now go back and read Matthew 6:1-18. Think of a movie or television show in which pastors or Christians are portrayed in a negative light. What negative stereotypes or behaviors are associated with these portrayals?

    Why do you think these negative perceptions exist?

4. Compare Matthew 6:1 to 5:16. Do you see a contradiction in Jesus's words? Why or why not?

DAY TWO

5. In Matthew 6, Jesus begins a discussion of acts of righteousness. Look back at this chapter and fill in the chart.

Act of Righteousness	What the Hypocrite Does	His Reward	What the Righteous Man Does	His Reward
Matthew 6:2-4				
Matthew 6:5-15				
Matthew 6:16-18				

> *² Thus, when you give to the needy, sound no trumpet before you, as the hypocrites do in the synagogues and in the streets, that they may be praised by others. Truly, I say to you, they have received their reward. ³ But when you give to the needy, do not let your left hand know what your right hand is doing, ⁴ so that your giving may be in secret. And your Father who sees in secret will reward you.*

MATTHEW 6:2-4

6. According to verse 2, what was wrong with the way the hypocrites were giving?

7. What do you think Jesus means by, "When you give to the needy, do not let your left hand know what your right hand is doing" (6:3)?

Why is this approach to giving important (6:2,4)?

8. What does a modern-day hypocritical giver look like? List some thoughts or examples.

9. Should all giving be done in secret? Why or why not?

10. **APPLY:** In what ways are you tempted to give hypocritically? What kinds of giving appeal to your pride?

How could you give to that same recipient in a God-honoring way?

DAY THREE

⁵ And when you pray, you must not be like the hypocrites. For they love to stand and pray in the synagogues and at the street corners, that they may be seen by others. Truly, I say to you, they have received their reward. ⁶ But when you pray, go into your room and shut the door and pray to your Father who is in secret. And your Father who sees in secret will reward you.

⁷ And when you pray, do not heap up empty phrases as the Gentiles do, for they think that they will be heard for their many words. ⁸ Do not be like them, for your Father knows what you need before you ask him.

MATTHEW 6:5-8

11. If your prayers were written down like those in the Psalms, what would those who read them learn about your concept of God?

12. According to Matthew 6:5, what was wrong with the prayers of the hypocrites?

Can a prayer request ever be used in a hypocritical way? Give an example.

READ MATTHEW 26:39-44.

13. What is the difference between the type of prayer described in Matthew 6:7 and the persistent prayer of Jesus?

14. How are we guilty of "heap[ing] up empty phrases" when we pray?

15. What do the following verses teach us about prayer?

John 9:31:

John 15:7:

If our Father knows what we need before we ask Him, why should we pray?

16. What aspect of the prayer of the hypocrite is most convicting to you? Would changing your words correct the problem? Explain your thoughts.

17. What makes our prayers acceptable to God?

DAY FOUR

> *¹⁶ And when you fast, do not look gloomy like the hypocrites, for they disfigure their faces that their fasting may be seen by others. Truly, I say to you, they have received their reward. ¹⁷ But when you fast, anoint your head and wash your face, ¹⁸ that your fasting may not be seen by others but by your Father who is in secret. And your Father who sees in secret will reward you.*

MATTHEW 6:16-18

18. What was the problem with the way the hypocrites of Jesus's day were fasting?

Fasting was practiced in many ways and for many reasons. A fast could be partial (see Dan. 10:2-3) or total (see Matt. 4:1-2), voluntary (see Dan. 9:3) or involuntary (see Dan. 6:18). The key concept in fasting was always the removal of something from everyday life in order to focus on God. For example, in Daniel 10, each time Daniel refused delicacies, meat, or wine during his fast, he was reminded of his position before God.

READ ISAIAH 58:1-12.

19. According to verses 1-4, why were the Israelites fasting?

20. Were they walking in righteousness before God? Explain.

21. In verse 5 we learn what the people were doing when they fasted. List some of these things.

22. According to verses 6-7, what kind of fast had God chosen?

23. In Isaiah 58:8-12, note each occurrence of "if" and "then." What are the end results of a godly fast?

24. **APPLY:** Why do you think fasting is not widely practiced today? Do you think it should be?

If so, what are some ways modern Christians can fast?

25. How do modern-day hypocrites abuse the discipline of fasting to receive glory for themselves rather than for God?

26. Note that Jesus says, "*when* you fast" (Matt. 6:16, emphasis mine). When do you fast? Pray and ask God to show you if there is something He would have you fast from that you might grow closer to Him. Write down some possible things from which you could fast.

DAY FIVE

The Lord's Prayer can be studied at length, and you should do that! But for our purpose of seeing the Sermon on the Mount as a whole, we will give it a brief treatment here.

> *9 Pray then like this: Our Father in heaven, hallowed be your name. 10 Your kingdom come, your will be done, on earth as it is in heaven. 11 Give us this day our daily bread, 12 and forgive us our debts, as we also have forgiven our debtors. 13 And lead us not into temptation, but deliver us from evil. 14 For if you forgive others their trespasses, your heavenly Father will also forgive you, 15 but if you do not forgive others their trespasses, neither will your Father forgive your trespasses.*

MATTHEW 6:9-15

27. Each of the following terms represent a key element in the Lord's Prayer. Look up each term in a dictionary or thesaurus, and write a brief definition.

Confession:

Submission:

Deliverance:

Petition:

Worship:

Allegiance:

28. Now, write each term beside the section of the Lord's Prayer to which you think it belongs. (Note them also in your copy of the text on page 182.)

Our Father in heaven,
hallowed be your name.

Your kingdom come,
your will be done,

on earth as it is in heaven.
Give us this day our daily bread,

and forgive us our debts,
as we also have forgiven our debtors.

And lead us not into temptation,
but deliver us from evil.

29. **READ PSALM 96.** What does this psalm teach us about the element of *worship* in prayer?

30. **READ 1 JOHN 5:14-15.** What do these verses teach us about the element of *submission* in prayer?

31. **READ JAMES 1:2-3,13-15.** How do these verses shape our interpretation of "Lead us not into temptation, but deliver us from evil"?

32. Matthew 6:14-15 reiterates one thought contained in the Lord's Prayer. Which one? Why do you think Jesus reiterates that particular idea?

33. The Lord's Prayer has been given to us as a model of how to pray. Of the six key elements of prayer Jesus highlights, which do you think is most frequently employed in prayers you hear at church and/or among Christians you know? Which is the least common? Why do you think this is so?

34. **APPLY:** Which of the six key elements of the Lord's Prayer needs more emphasis in your prayers?

WRAP-UP

What impacted you most in this week's passage from the Sermon on the Mount? What are the words of Jesus on giving, praying, and fasting asking of you personally?

INTRODUCTORY QUESTION: What snack food do you find irresistible? What is your "food kryptonite"?

1. **REFLECT:** (question 7, p. 100) What do you think Jesus means by, "When you give to the needy, do not let your left hand know what your right hand is doing" (6:3)? Why is this approach to giving important (6:2,4)?

   APPLY: (question 10, p. 100) In what ways are you tempted to give hypocritically? What kinds of giving appeal to your pride? How could you give to that same recipient in a God-honoring way?

2. **REFLECT:** (question 12, p. 101) According to Matthew 6:5, what was wrong with the prayers of the hypocrites?

   APPLY: How are you tempted toward hypocrisy in your own prayers? What situations or circumstances make genuine prayer hardest for you?

3. **REFLECT:** (question 23, p. 104) According to Isaiah 58:8-12, what are the end results of a godly fast?

APPLY: (question 24, p. 104) Why do you think fasting is not widely practiced today? Do you think it should be? If so, what are some ways modern Christians can fast?

4. **REFLECT:** (question 33, p. 108) The Lord's Prayer has been given to us as a model of how to pray. Of the six key elements of prayer Jesus highlights, which do you think is most frequently employed in prayers you hear at church and/or among Christians you know? Which is the least common? Why do you think this is so?

APPLY: (question 34, p. 109) Which of the six key elements of the Lord's Prayer needs more emphasis in your prayers?

5. **WRAP-UP:** (p. 109) What impacted you most in this week's passage from the Sermon on the Mount? What are the words of Jesus on giving, praying, and fasting asking of you personally?

Secret Righteousness

Watch the teaching video for Week Six. Use the space provided to take notes.

To access the video teaching sessions, use the instructions in the back of your workbook.

After the video concludes, close your study in prayer. Praise God that He is worthy of our obedience, both public and private. Ask Him to help you develop the habits of secret praying, giving, and fasting. Ask Him for the wisdom to know when to show and when to hide your acts of obedience. Thank God that He does not merely command us to pray, but that He instructs us how. Thank Him that He sees you in the secret place.

week seven

WHERE YOUR TREASURE IS

Last week Jesus addressed the way we give, pray, and fast—three righteous acts intended to turn our attention heavenward. Because we are lovers of self, we can turn even that which should humble us into that which becomes a source of pride. We can perform our acts of righteousness not to bring glory to God, but to ourselves. We were reminded that God is a God who sees us in the secret place, a truth that is both a caution and a beautiful assurance. And we were given a pattern for prayer to help us orient our hearts humbly toward our Father in heaven.

This week Jesus turns our attention earthward, challenging us to think differently about how we relate to the money, possessions, and other earthly treasures that consume our time and energy. Not surprisingly, Jesus will address the worry and anxiety inevitably associated with storing up treasures on earth. Most of us battle worry, either during a stressful season of life or as a constant nagging companion lurking in the back of our consciousness. Jesus intends to free us from the misconception that worry and anxiety are normal in the life of a disciple, and to gently direct us to a better way: trusting in an infinitely good Father who knows and supplies perfectly the needs of His children.

DAY ONE

READ MATTHEW 5:1–7:29 ON PAGES 176–187.

1. As you read, (circle) each occurrence of the words "reward" or "treasure" with a yellow pencil or marker. Based on how this concept is presented throughout the sermon, what kind of reward or treasure should we set our hope on?

2. Take fifteen minutes to practice memorizing the passage you chose last week.

NOW READ MATTHEW 6:19-34.

3. How does this week's passage follow logically on the heels of the passage we focused on in Week Six (see Matt. 6:1-18)?

4. Summarize the main idea of Matthew 6:19-24.

5. Summarize the main idea of Matthew 6:25-34.

Now transfer your summary statements to the margin of your copy of the text on pages 176–187, writing them next to the section they summarize.

DAY TWO

> *¹⁹ Do not lay up for yourselves treasures on earth, where moth and rust destroy and where thieves break in and steal, ²⁰ but lay up for yourselves treasures in heaven, where neither moth nor rust destroys and where thieves do not break in and steal. ²¹ For where your treasure is, there your heart will be also.*

MATTHEW 6:19-21

6. Why do you think Jesus says we should lay up heavenly treasures instead of earthly ones?

How, practically, can we do this? List some thoughts below.

7. Is Jesus teaching that it is wrong for the Christian to possess personal property, savings, or insurance policies? Why or why not?

READ PROVERBS 30:1-9.

8. What two things did Agur request of God with regard to riches?

9. Compare Proverbs 30:8 in the ESV and NIV. What did Agur ask God to give him "only" (NIV)?

How might this add to your understanding (and use) of the Lord's Prayer?

READ REVELATION 3:14-22.

10. What does verse 17 tell us about the source of the apathy of the Laodiceans?

11. What three conditions listed in verse 17 does verse 18 counsel them to remedy by seeking God?

12. Can you find each of these three conditions addressed in Matthew 6:19-34? Go back to your responses in question 11 and note the relevant verse(s) next to each condition.

13. **READ 2 PETER 3:10-14.** What do these verses teach us about material versus spiritual possessions?

How does verse 11 suggest that we lay up treasures in heaven?

14. **APPLY**: What do you think is meant by the phrase, "Where your treasure is, there your heart will be also" (Matt. 6:21)?

Restate Matthew 6:21 in your own words.

15. **NOW READ PSALM 24:1-2 IN THE ESV AND THE NIV.** How can you live in the light of these verses so that your heart and treasure are where they should be?

DAY THREE

²² The eye is the lamp of the body. So, if your eye is healthy, your whole body will be full of light, ²³ but if your eye is bad, your whole body will be full of darkness. If then the light in you is darkness, how great is the darkness!

²⁴ No one can serve two masters, for either he will hate the one and love the other, or he will be devoted to the one and despise the other. You cannot serve God and money.

MATTHEW 6:22-24

16. In Week Four we studied a passage in Job in which Job had made a special covenant. Note Job's words in Job 31:1:

    "I have made a covenant _____ ."

    What role do you think the eyes play in the committing of sin?

17. **READ GENESIS 3:1-6.** What process does Eve go through in verse 6?

    1. She _____ the fruit.

    2. She *desired* the fruit.

    3. She _____ the fruit.

    4. She _____ the fruit.

    5. She _____ the fruit to Adam.

18. When Joshua is commanded to take the city of Jericho, God gives specific instructions about what to do with the spoils (see Josh. 6:18-19). Achan, one of his commanders, disobeys these instructions (see Josh. 7:1). **READ JOSHUA 7:19-25** and note the similarities between Achan's story and Eve's story.

19. **READ 2 SAMUEL 11:1-5,14-17,26-27.** What similarities can you find between David's story and those you have just studied?

20. Read the following passages, and note what each teaches about our eyes.

    2 Corinthians 4:18:

    Hebrews 12:2 (NIV):

    1 John 2:15-17:

21. How does 1 John 2:15-17 relate to Matthew 6:24?

22. Restate Matthew 6:22-23 in your own words.

23. **APPLY:** In Matthew 6:24, Jesus warns that you cannot serve two masters. Many people hold down two jobs to support a family. In effect, they serve two masters. How is what Jesus is saying different from this scenario (i.e., what does the term *master* mean to Him)?

What worldly "master" is fighting for your loyalties in your daily life? On what master have you "fixed your eyes"? Write it below. Pray and ask God to help you see and serve Him rather than temporal pleasures or pursuits.

DAY FOUR

Therefore I tell you, do not be anxious about your life . . .

MATTHEW 6:25

READ MATTHEW 6:25-30.

24. What two images from nature does Jesus use to illustrate why we
should not be anxious for anything?

What is His point in choosing these two images?

25. What do you think food and clothing represent in this passage? Check the
paraphrase you think fits most closely with Jesus's meaning in 6:28.

☐ Do not worry about which foods to eat and which clothes to wear.

☐ Do not worry about having enough food to eat or enough clothes to wear.

Do we usually spend our time worrying about basic needs or about
"extras"? Explain your response.

NOW REREAD MATTHEW 6:25-30.

26. How will the treasures and masters we choose in verses 19-24 impact our ability to live lives free from worry?

27. In verse 30, Jesus refers to His listeners as "O you of little faith." What relationship is Jesus indicating exists between worry and faith?

28. Does relying solely on God's provision relieve us of the responsibility of working? Read 2 Thessalonians 3:6-15. How does Paul answer this question?

29. What things consume the most time and energy in your life? Write them below. We will revisit your answer on Day Five.

30. **APPLY:** What are you most anxious about? List those things here.

READ 1 PETER 5:6-7. How can you apply these verses to your list of anxieties?

Pray and ask God to teach you the humility of casting your anxieties on Him.

DAY FIVE

31 Therefore do not be anxious, saying, "What shall we eat?" or "What shall we drink?" or "What shall we wear?" 32 For the Gentiles seek after all these things, and your heavenly Father knows that you need them all. 33 But seek first the kingdom of God and his righteousness, and all these things will be added to you.

34 Therefore do not be anxious about tomorrow, for tomorrow will be anxious for itself. Sufficient for the day is its own trouble.

MATTHEW 6:31-34

31. **COMPARE MATTHEW 6:31-34 IN THE ESV AND THE NIV.** Give examples of how people today "run after all these things" (v. 32, NIV) that Jesus mentions.

32. **READ MATTHEW 25:41-45.** God promises to feed and clothe His children, but many today are in need of these things. Why might this be the case?

33. What does it mean to seek first His kingdom?

To seek first His righteousness?

34. **APPLY:** List below your top three priorities in sentence form.

In yesterday's lesson we asked ourselves what things consume the most time and energy in our lives. Does your list of top priorities reflect where your time and energy are spent? Explain your thoughts.

Pray and ask God to help your priorities and your efforts align.

WRAP-UP

What impacted you most in this week's passage from the Sermon on the Mount? What are the words of Jesus regarding treasures and worry asking of you personally?

INTRODUCTORY QUESTION: Describe the best gift you have received and why it is your favorite.

1. REFLECT: Look back over questions 4 and 5 on Day One (p. 116). Summarize the main ideas of Matthew 6:19-34.

APPLY: (question 14, p. 119) What do you think is meant by the phrase, "Where your treasure is, there your heart will be also" (Matt. 6:21)?

2. REFLECT: Look back over questions 17, 18, and 19 on Day Three. When you "see" something that tempts you, what can you do to stop the process of sin seen in these Scripture passages? In other words, what should Eve, Achan, and David have done differently?

APPLY: (question 23, p. 122) In Matthew 6:24, Jesus warns that you cannot serve two masters. Many people hold down two jobs to support a family. In effect, they serve two masters. How is what Jesus is saying different from this scenario (i.e., what does the term *master* mean to Him)? What worldly "master" is fighting for your loyalties in your daily life? On what master have you "fixed your eyes"? Write it below. Pray and ask God to help you see and serve Him rather than temporal pleasures or pursuits.

3. REFLECT: (question 26, p. 124) How will the treasures and masters we choose in Matthew 6:19-24 impact our ability to live lives free from worry?

   APPLY: (question 30, p. 125) What are you most anxious about? How can you apply 1 Peter 5:6-7 to your list of anxieties?

4. REFLECT: (question 33, p. 126) What does it mean to seek first His kingdom? His righteousness?

   APPLY: (question 34, p. 127) In Day Four we asked ourselves what things consume the most time and energy in our lives. Does your list of top priorities reflect where your time and energy are spent? Explain your thoughts.

5. WRAP-UP: (p. 127) What impacted you most in this week's passage from the Sermon on the Mount? What are the words of Jesus regarding treasures and worry asking of you personally?

Where Your Treasure Is

Watch the teaching video for Week Seven. Use the space provided to take notes.

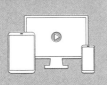

To access the video teaching sessions, use the instructions in the back of your workbook.

After the video concludes, close your study in prayer. Praise God that by His grace you can invest now in things of eternal significance. Ask Him to help you have one treasure, one vision, one Master. Confess your worries and anxieties as unbelief. Thank Him that He knows your needs and takes pleasure in meeting them.

week eight

DO UNTO
OTHERS

Last week we learned that there were two places we can store up treasure: in heaven or on earth. We learned that there are two masters we have to choose between: God or self. And we learned that there are two directions we can fix our gaze: on what is good or on what is evil. Jesus took great care to instruct us on choosing the better thing. Connecting worry to the pursuit of the wrong treasure, master, and vision, He admonished us not to worry about ourselves, what we would eat, drink, or wear. These matters, He assured, can be trusted to our good Father in heaven.

This week we will consider the way we view the sin of others, as well as our own sin. "Judge not, that you be not judged" (Matt. 7:1) is one of those verses everyone, Christian or non-Christian, likes to quote freely. But do we quote it in a way that is faithful to the teaching of Jesus or in a way that serves our own interests? And what about asking, seeking, and knocking? Does Jesus mean for us to understand that God needs to be convinced of our earnestness when we pray? And what about "Do to others what you would have them do to you" (Matt. 7:12, NIV)? Is the Golden Rule a command to treat others fairly, or is it perhaps something more than that? As He has done thus far in the Sermon on the Mount, Jesus will ask of us a deeper obedience than we might otherwise offer. May God give us ears to hear His words afresh this week.

DAY ONE

READ MATTHEW 5:1–7:29 ON PAGES 176–187.

1. Take fifteen minutes to work on committing to memory the passage you chose (p. 98). If you have already memorized your chosen passage, ask God to show you other passages you could begin to learn.

2. Look back at Day One of Week Seven (p. 116). Recopy your summary statements for the following passages.

    Matthew 6:19-24:

    Matthew 6:25-34:

NOW READ MATTHEW 7:1-12.

3. As you read, mark every direct command in this section of the text. Mark each "do" with a green wavy underline. Mark each "don't" with a red jagged underline. If you love annotating, feel free to do this for the entire Sermon on the Mount for commands both implied and stated.

4. How does this week's passage follow logically on the heels of Matthew 6:19-34?

DAY TWO

¹ Judge not, that you be not judged. ² For with the judgment you pronounce you will be judged, and with the measure you use it will be measured to you. ³ Why do you see the speck that is in your brother's eye, but do not notice the log that is in your own eye? ⁴ Or how can you say to your brother, "Let me take the speck out of your eye," when there is the log in your own eye? ⁵ You hypocrite, first take the log out of your own eye, and then you will see clearly to take the speck out of your brother's eye.

MATTHEW 7:1-5

5. Look back through the Sermon on the Mount, and list below passages that express a similar thought to that of Matthew 7:1-2.

6. In Matthew 7:3-5, Jesus uses a colorful illustration to teach a basic truth about human nature. What are the similarities and differences between a speck of sawdust and a log? What does each represent? Fill in the chart below.

	Speck of Sawdust	Log
Same		
Different		
Meaning		

7. Consider Jesus's audience for the Sermon on the Mount. Next to each group of "listeners" below, note why you think Jesus chose this particular topic. What did He want to communicate to each group and why?

   The disciples:

   The crowds:

   The scribes and Pharisees:

8. In Matthew 7:4-5, whose eye was it that contained a speck of sawdust?

   Why do you think Jesus uses this term?

9. Is Jesus commanding that we are never to judge others? Read the following verses and note the main thought of each.

    James 5:19-20:

    Galatians 6:1:

    Based on these verses, what type of judging is Jesus warning against in Matthew 7:1-5?

10. **READ ROMANS 2:1-6,21-24.** How do these verses add to your understanding of Matthew 7:1-5?

11. **APPLY:** Upon whom are you guilty of passing judgment for a sin that is also your own? Confess your own sin to God. Ask Him to help you extend grace instead of judgment to those who offend you with similar sins to your own.

DAY THREE

*Do not give dogs what is holy, and do not
throw your pearls before pigs, lest they trample
them underfoot and turn to attack you.*

MATTHEW 7:6

To the Jew, both dogs and pigs were considered unclean animals. The "dogs"
Jesus refers to in His analogy would not have been domesticated animals, but
wild and ferocious animals that scavenged and stole to survive.

12. **READ PHILIPPIANS 3:2-3 AND 3:17-19.** Who are the "dogs" in this passage?

How would they fit the statement Jesus makes in Matthew 7:6?

13. **READ 2 PETER 2:1-3 AND 2:21-22.** Who are described as "dogs" and "pigs"
in this chapter?

How would they fit the statement that Jesus makes in verse 6?

How are they different from the "dogs" described in Philippians 3?

What type of behavior is represented in the analogy found in
2 Peter 2:22?

14. If we are to "judge not" (7:1), how are we to discern who is a dog or a pig?

15. What do you think are the "holy" things or "pearls" we are not to offer to "dogs" and "pigs" in Matthew 7:6?

16. Read the following verses and note how they relate to Matthew 7:6.

    Proverbs 23:9:

    Proverbs 9:7-9:

    2 Corinthians 2:14-16:

17. Now rewrite Matthew 7:6 in your own words.

18. **APPLY:** Have you ever been met with total rejection after sharing the gospel? How can we know whether we are dealing with pigs and dogs or with someone who might respond to the gospel at a later time?

DAY FOUR

⁷ Ask, and it will be given to you; seek, and you will find; knock, and it will be opened to you. ⁸ For everyone who asks receives, and the one who seeks finds, and to the one who knocks it will be opened.

MATTHEW 7:7-8

19. What assurance does Jesus give those who ask, seek, and knock?

20. Why do you think Jesus offers this type of encouragement at this point in His discourse?

21. Based on the topics Jesus has covered thus far, what things might the disciples be moved to request with urgency and persistence?

22. "Ask, and it will be given to you" (7:7) could be taken to mean that God grants whatever we ask. Read the following passages, and form a response to this misconception.

James 4:1-3:

Proverbs 28:9:

23. Note the progression in the three actions Jesus encourages. How does each action build on the idea of how to request things from God? Paraphrase the action you think each implies.

Ask:

Seek:

Knock:

24. The tense of each of the three verbs indicates a continuous and ongoing action (i.e., keep asking, keep seeking, keep knocking). Why does Jesus teach that prayer requires persistence?

25. If God does not need to be encouraged, convinced, or coerced, why might He not answer a request made only once?

26. Is there something for which you have kept asking, kept seeking, and kept knocking? How are Jesus's words an encouragement to you?

DAY FIVE

⁹ Or which one of you, if his son asks him for bread, will give him a stone? ¹⁰ Or if he asks for a fish, will give him a serpent? ¹¹ If you then, who are evil, know how to give good gifts to your children, how much more will your Father who is in heaven give good things to those who ask him!

¹² So whatever you wish that others would do to you, do also to them, for this is the Law and the Prophets.

MATTHEW 7:9-12

27. **READ LUKE 11:1-13.** In this corresponding passage to Matthew 7:9-12, Jesus gives an illustration of a man going to his neighbor to ask for bread. How does this illustration expand your understanding of how God responds to our requests?

28. In Matthew 7:11, to whom is Jesus referring when He says, "If *you*, then, who are evil . . . " (emphasis mine)?

29. Based on Matthew 7:9-11, does God give as a parent gives to a child? Explain.

30. What is the name commonly given to Matthew 7:12?

31. The Jewish Talmud (sacred writings) commanded: "What is hateful to you, do not do unto your neighbor."[1] Confucius commanded his followers: "Do not to others what you would not wish done to you."[2] How does Jesus's command go beyond those of the Talmud and Confucius?

32. **COMPARE MATTHEW 7:12 IN THE ESV AND NIV.** In what sense does the Golden Rule sum up the Law and the Prophets?

33. **APPLY:** Is there someone toward whom you hesitate to demonstrate the Golden Rule? Who?

---

1. "Shabbat 31a," The William Davidson Talmud (Korea – Steinsaltz), Sefaria, accessed May 8, 2023, https://www.sefaria.org/Shabbat.31a.4?lang=bi.
2. Confucius, *The Analects*, Trans. D.C. Lau (New York: Penguin Putnam, 1979), Book 5.

Why do you think it is so difficult to treat that particular person the way you would like to be treated?

How could you ask God to change your thinking about that person (or about yourself) to make it easier for you to treat him or her better?

WRAP-UP

What impacted you most in this week's passage from the Sermon on the Mount? What are the words of Jesus on judging, persistent requesting, and doing to others asking of you personally?

INTRODUCTORY QUESTION: What did you consider to be the most valuable thing you owned when you were a child? When you were a teenager? How about now?

1. REFLECT: (question 10, p. 137) Read Romans 2:1-6,21-24. How do these verses add to your understanding of Matthew 7:1-5?

APPLY: Which sins or categories of sins are you most likely to judge others for that you also commit?

2. REFLECT: (questions 14–15, p. 139) If we are to "judge not" (7:1), how are we to discern who is a dog or a pig? What do you think are the "holy" things or "pearls" we are not to offer to "dogs" and "pigs" in 7:6?

APPLY: (question 18, p. 139) Have you ever been met with total rejection after sharing the gospel? How can we know whether we are dealing with pigs and dogs or with someone who might respond to the gospel at a later time?

3. REFLECT: Read Matthew 7:7. Has your understanding of this frequently quoted verse changed as you have studied it within the context of the Sermon on the Mount? If yes, how? (question 21, p. 140) Based on the topics Jesus has covered thus far, what things might the disciples be moved to request with urgency and persistence?

APPLY: How has studying the Sermon on the Mount as a whole influenced that for which you will ask, seek, and knock?

4. **REFLECT:** (question 32, p. 144) Compare Matthew 7:12 in the ESV and NIV. In what sense does the Golden Rule sum up the Law and the Prophets?

APPLY: (question 33, pp. 144–145) Is there someone toward whom you hesitate to demonstrate the Golden Rule? Who? How could you ask God to change your thinking about that person (or about yourself) to make it easier for you to treat him or her better?

5. **WRAP-UP:** (p. 145) What impacted you most in this week's passage from the Sermon on the Mount? What are the words of Jesus on judging, persistent requesting, and doing to others asking of you personally?

Do Unto Others

Watch the teaching video for Week Eight. Use the space provided to take notes.

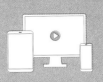

To access the video teaching sessions, use the instructions in the back of your workbook.

After the video concludes, close your study in prayer. Praise God that He is a "much more" Father. Ask Him to help you learn to see your own sin before you look for sin in another. Ask Him to help you trust Him as the Giver of all good things, and to increase your boldness to ask, seek, and knock for your spiritual daily bread. Thank Him that He has set His preferential love on you as a seal.

week nine

A FOUNDATION THAT ENDURES

Last week we distinguished between two kinds of "judging others." We learned that while worldly judgment seeks to condemn and reject, godly judgment seeks to heal and restore. We saw that we must be careful not to subject the gospel to ridicule by offering it to those who have repeatedly and adamantly rejected it. We learned that our heavenly Father is a "much more" Father who does not deny His children their earnest requests for spiritual daily bread. And we learned that the Golden Rule asks us to show love to others not merely as they deserve, but beyond what they deserve. It is a call to love preferentially as Christ loves us.

This week we will listen as Jesus masterfully draws His sermon to its conclusion. Like any good teacher, Jesus ends by asking His listeners to respond to His message. He poses a series of contrasts that will challenge them to consider whether they resemble a citizen of heaven or a citizen of earth: there are two kinds of gates. Which one will you choose? There are two kinds of teachers. Which one will you listen to? There are two kinds of servants. Which one will you be? There are two kinds of foundations. On which will you build?

If ever a sermon required a response, surely it is this one. Jesus's listeners did not know how His earthly ministry would end, but we do. If they listened and were amazed, how much more amazed ought we be, as those who live in light of the finished work of Christ? As you consider what Jesus's words asked of His original hearers, consider what they are asking of you.

DAY ONE

READ MATTHEW 5:1–7:29 IN THE NIV TRANSLATION.

1. Recite aloud your passage that you committed to memory during this study.

2. After repeated readings, if you could choose one verse as the key for the Sermon on the Mount, which one would you choose? Why?

NOW READ MATTHEW 7:13-29.

3. Summarize this week's passage into two or three sections, writing your summary statements in the margin of your copy of the text on pages 185–187 next to the section they summarize.

4. How does this week's passage follow logically on the heels of Matthew 7:1-12?

DAY TWO

¹³ Enter by the narrow gate. For the gate is wide and the way is easy that leads to destruction, and those who enter by it are many. ¹⁴ For the gate is narrow and the way is hard that leads to life, and those who find it are few.

MATTHEW 7:13-14

5. In verses 13-14, Jesus describes two gates and two roads. Read these verses in the ESV (above) and NIV.

   How are the two gates different?

   How are the two ways or roads different?

6. In what regard is the gate of Christianity small?

   In what regard is the road of Christianity narrow?

READ LUKE 13:22-30.

7. In this similar passage, what is the question that is asked of Jesus?

   How does Jesus answer?

8. In Luke 13:24, how might someone seek to enter the narrow gate and not be able to?

9. **APPLY:** How have you heard people react to Jesus's statement that there is only one true gate, road, and destination?

   Why do you think they react this way?

10. How narrow is the gate Jesus mentions? Look up the following verses and note what each says.

John 3:36:

John 10:9:

Acts 4:12:

1 Timothy 2:5:

1 John 5:12:

In what way is the truth of the narrow gate and way a warning to you?

How is it a source of assurance?

DAY THREE

> [15] *Beware of false prophets, who come to you in sheep's clothing but inwardly are ravenous wolves.* [16] *You will recognize them by their fruits. Are grapes gathered from thornbushes, or figs from thistles?* [17] *So, every healthy tree bears good fruit, but the diseased tree bears bad fruit.* [18] *A healthy tree cannot bear bad fruit, nor can a diseased tree bear good fruit.* [19] *Every tree that does not bear good fruit is cut down and thrown into the fire.* [20] *Thus you will recognize them by their fruits.*

MATTHEW 7:15-20

11. Why do you think Jesus moves from a discussion of the wide and narrow ways to a warning about false prophets?

12. What types of sheep's clothing would false prophets wear today?

13. How is a false prophet like a ferocious wolf?

14. If we are to recognize a false prophet by his fruit, what types of fruit should we look for?

15. **READ MATTHEW 12:33-35**. What does this passage reveal as a type of fruit by which a false prophet can be identified?

16. **ACCORDING TO HEBREWS 5:11-14,** how can we know if the words of a teacher are true?

17. **READ 1 JOHN 4:1-6.** Are we responsible to discern between the Spirit of truth and a spirit of error? What does this passage tell us about discerning which is which?

18. **APPLY:** Give some examples of popular false teaching among Christian circles and secular circles. How can we be careful to identify false teaching?

READ HEBREWS 4:12. What sharp implement is provided to us for the purpose of cutting down a tree that "bears bad fruit" (Matt. 7:17)?

How skilled are you in using this tool? How can you become better at using it to discern truth from error?

DAY FOUR

²¹ Not everyone who says to me, "Lord, Lord," will enter the kingdom of heaven, but the one who does the will of my Father who is in heaven. ²² On that day many will say to me, "Lord, Lord, did we not prophesy in your name, and cast out demons in your name, and do many mighty works in your name?" ²³ And then will I declare to them, "I never knew you; depart from me, you workers of lawlessness."

MATTHEW 7:21-23

19. What do you think the statement, "Lord, Lord" is supposed to imply about the attitude of the one who speaks it?

20. The people described in verses 21-23 perform admirable deeds and speak admirable words. Why does Jesus condemn them?

21. Who has led the people astray? (Consider Matthew 7:15-20.)

22. According to Matthew 7:21, who will enter the kingdom of heaven?

Does this mean that salvation is earned by what we do? Why or why not?

23. What sort of person is described as not gaining admittance to the kingdom of heaven?

24. Apparently, someone without saving faith can perform some amazing works in the name of Jesus. What three examples does Jesus give in Matthew 7:22?

25. Why do you think God allows unbelievers to do remarkable things in His name? Give your best guess, and then look up Philippians 1:15-18 to see Paul's thoughts on this subject.

26. **APPLY:** Have you ever benefited spiritually from the ministry of someone who later turned out to be a false prophet? Describe that time.

How did that experience change the way you viewed people in ministry?

How did it change the way you viewed God?

DAY FIVE

²⁴ Everyone then who hears these words of mine and does them will be like a wise man who built his house on the rock. ²⁵ And the rain fell, and the floods came, and the winds blew and beat on that house, but it did not fall, because it had been founded on the rock. ²⁶ And everyone who hears these words of mine and does not do them will be like a foolish man who built his house on the sand. ²⁷ And the rain fell, and the floods came, and the winds blew and beat against that house, and it fell, and great was the fall of it.

MATTHEW 7:24-27

27. **LOOK CLOSELY AT VERSE 24.** What two conditions must be met to be like the man who built on a rock?

28. How are the two houses in Jesus's illustration similar?

How are they different?

29. At what point would the difference(s) be revealed between the two houses?

30. Based on Matthew 7:24-27, label the picture below with what you think each part of the story about the wise man's house represents.

31. **APPLY:** What are some examples of rain, flood, and wind that come into our lives?

Are these events always unexpected, uninvited, or undeserved? Explain.

Can you identify with the word picture Jesus paints in these verses? Describe a time in your life when you found Christ to be a sure foundation.

32. **APPLY:** Matthew 7:28 says that when Jesus finished speaking, the crowds were "astonished at his teaching." Has any particular part of the Sermon on the Mount astonished you? Which one(s)? Why?

WRAP-UP

What impacted you most in this week's passage from the Sermon on the Mount? What are the words of Jesus asking of you personally?

INTRODUCTORY QUESTION: If you could build your dream home, where would it be and what would it look like?

1. REFLECT: Look back over questions 5 and 6 on Day Two (p. 153). Specifically, how is the gate of Christianity small and the road narrow?

APPLY: (question 9, p. 154) How have you heard people react to Jesus's statement that there is only one true gate, road, and destination? Why do you think they react this way?

2. REFLECT: (question 16, p. 157) According to Hebrews 5:11-14, how can we know if the words of a teacher are true?

APPLY: (question 18, p. 158) Give some examples of popular false teaching among Christian circles and secular circles. How can we be careful to identify false teaching? Read Hebrews 4:12. What sharp implement is provided to us for the purpose of cutting down a tree that "bears bad fruit" (Matt. 7:17)? How skilled are you in using this tool? How can you become better at using it to discern truth from error?

3. REFLECT: (question 22, p. 160) According to Matthew 7:21, who will enter the kingdom of heaven? Does this mean that salvation is earned by what we do? Why or why not?

APPLY: (question 26, p. 161) Have you ever benefited spiritually from the ministry of someone who later turned out to be a false prophet? Describe that time. How did that experience change the way you viewed people in ministry? How did it change the way you viewed God?

4. REFLECT: (questions 28–29, pp. 162–163) How are the two houses in Jesus's illustration similar? How are they different? At what point would the difference(s) be revealed between the two houses?

APPLY: (question 31, p. 164) What are some examples of rain, flood, and wind that come into our lives? Are these events always unexpected, uninvited, or undeserved? Describe a time in your life when you found Christ to be a sure foundation.

5. WRAP-UP: (p. 165) What impacted you most in this week's passage from the Sermon on the Mount? What are the words of Jesus asking of you personally?

A Foundation That Endures

Watch the teaching video for Week Nine. Use the space provided to take notes.

To access the video teaching sessions, use the instructions in the back of your workbook.

After the video concludes, close your study in prayer. Praise God for the faithful record of Jesus's words in Matthew 5–7. Thank Him for the firm foundation they represent. Ask God to help you build the house of your faith into a dwelling fit for the Lord Himself. Ask Him to help you remember your own amazement at what the Sermon on the Mount contains, and to be changed by it. Thank God that Jesus lived out the "deeper obedience" of His sermon, as both our perfect example and our perfect atoning sacrifice. Thank Him that though the grass withers and the flowers fade, the Word of the Lord stands forever (see Isa. 40:8).

WRAP-UP

For the past nine weeks, you have had the opportunity to study Jesus's Sermon on the Mount as it was originally intended—as one cohesive message that details what the life of a Christ-follower should look like. Take some time to reflect on what you will take away from this study. Begin by reading through Matthew 5–7 one last time. As you do, pay special attention to what stands out most in your mind from your time spent with this teaching from Jesus.

READ STRAIGHT THROUGH MATTHEW 5–7.

As you read, think back on what you've learned throughout your study. Answer the following questions.

1. What impacted you most through your time in the Sermon on the Mount?

What have you learned about the character of God through this study?

What are the words of Jesus asking of you personally?

2. How has the Holy Spirit used the Sermon on the Mount to convict you of sin? What thoughts, words, or actions has He shown you that need to be redeemed? What do you need to stop doing?

3. How has the Holy Spirit used the Sermon on the Mount to train you in righteousness? What disciplines has He given you a desire to pursue? What do you need to start doing?

4. How has the Holy Spirit used the Sermon on the Mount to encourage you? What cause to celebrate has Jesus's teaching imprinted on your heart?

5. What verse or passage from Matthew 5–7 stands out most in your mind after nine weeks of study? Why?

Close in prayer. Thank God for giving us this teaching from Jesus that clearly articulates how a disciple of Christ is to think, speak, and act in the world. Thank God for challenging us to think differently about repentance, salvation, and sanctification. Ask Him to make you a disciple who "hears these words of [His] and does them." Thank Him for the example of Jesus, who modeled kingdom living perfectly for us.

Matthew 5–7

MATTHEW 5

The Sermon on the Mount

[1] Seeing the crowds, he went up on the mountain, and when he sat down, his disciples came to him.

The Beatitudes

[2] And he opened his mouth and taught them, saying:

[3] "Blessed are the poor in spirit, for theirs is the kingdom of heaven.

[4] "Blessed are those who mourn, for they shall be comforted.

[5] "Blessed are the meek, for they shall inherit the earth.

[6] "Blessed are those who hunger and thirst for righteousness, for they shall be satisfied.

[7] "Blessed are the merciful, for they shall receive mercy.

[8] "Blessed are the pure in heart, for they shall see God.

[9] "Blessed are the peacemakers, for they shall be called sons of God.

[10] "Blessed are those who are persecuted for righteousness' sake, for theirs is the kingdom of heaven.

11 "Blessed are you when others revile you and persecute you and utter all kinds of evil against you falsely on my account. 12 Rejoice and be glad, for your reward is great in heaven, for so they persecuted the prophets who were before you.

Salt and Light

13 "You are the salt of the earth, but if salt has lost its taste, how shall its saltiness be restored? It is no longer good for anything except to be thrown out and trampled under people's feet.

14 "You are the light of the world. A city set on a hill cannot be hidden. 15 Nor do people light a lamp and put it under a basket, but on a stand, and it gives light to all in the house. 16 In the same way, let your light shine before others, so that they may see your good works and give glory to your Father who is in heaven.

Christ Came to Fulfill the Law

17 "Do not think that I have come to abolish the Law or the Prophets; I have not come to abolish them but to fulfill them. 18 For truly, I say to you, until heaven and earth pass away, not an iota, not a dot, will pass from the Law until all is accomplished. 19 Therefore whoever relaxes one of the least of these commandments and teaches others to do the same will be called least in the kingdom of heaven, but whoever does

them and teaches them will be called great in the kingdom of heaven. [20] For I tell you, unless your righteousness exceeds that of the scribes and Pharisees, you will never enter the kingdom of heaven.

Anger

[21] "You have heard that it was said to those of old, 'You shall not murder; and whoever murders will be liable to judgment.' [22] But I say to you that everyone who is angry with his brother will be liable to judgment; whoever insults his brother will be liable to the council; and whoever says, 'You fool!' will be liable to the hell of fire. [23] So if you are offering your gift at the altar and there remember that your brother has something against you, [24] leave your gift there before the altar and go. First be reconciled to your brother, and then come and offer your gift. [25] Come to terms quickly with your accuser while you are going with him to court, lest your accuser hand you over to the judge, and the judge to the guard, and you be put in prison. [26] Truly, I say to you, you will never get out until you have paid the last penny.

Lust

[27] "You have heard that it was said, 'You shall not commit adultery.' [28] But I say to you that everyone who looks at a woman with lustful intent has already committed adultery

with her in his heart. [29] If your right eye causes you to sin, tear it out and throw it away. For it is better that you lose one of your members than that your whole body be thrown into hell. [30] And if your right hand causes you to sin, cut it off and throw it away. For it is better that you lose one of your members than that your whole body go into hell.

Divorce

[31] "It was also said, 'Whoever divorces his wife, let him give her a certificate of divorce.' [32] But I say to you that everyone who divorces his wife, except on the ground of sexual immorality, makes her commit adultery, and whoever marries a divorced woman commits adultery.

Oaths

[33] "Again you have heard that it was said to those of old, 'You shall not swear falsely, but shall perform to the Lord what you have sworn.' [34] But I say to you, Do not take an oath at all, either by heaven, for it is the throne of God, [35] or by the earth, for it is his footstool, or by Jerusalem, for it is the city of the great King. [36] And do not take an oath by your head, for you cannot make one hair white or black. [37] Let what you say be simply 'Yes' or 'No'; anything more than this comes from evil.

Retaliation

38 "You have heard that it was said, 'An eye for an eye and a tooth for a tooth.' 39 But I say to you, Do not resist the one who is evil. But if anyone slaps you on the right cheek, turn to him the other also. 40 And if anyone would sue you and take your tunic, let him have your cloak as well. 41 And if anyone forces you to go one mile, go with him two miles. 42 Give to the one who begs from you, and do not refuse the one who would borrow from you.

Love Your Enemies

43 "You have heard that it was said, 'You shall love your neighbor and hate your enemy.' 44 But I say to you, Love your enemies and pray for those who persecute you, 45 so that you may be sons of your Father who is in heaven. For he makes his sun rise on the evil and on the good, and sends rain on the just and on the unjust. 46 For if you love those who love you, what reward do you have? Do not even the tax collectors do the same? 47 And if you greet only your brothers, what more are you doing than others? Do not even the Gentiles do the same? 48 You therefore must be perfect, as your heavenly Father is perfect.

MATTHEW 6

Giving to the Needy

[1] "Beware of practicing your righteousness before other people in order to be seen by them, for then you will have no reward from your Father who is in heaven.

[2] "Thus, when you give to the needy, sound no trumpet before you, as the hypocrites do in the synagogues and in the streets, that they may be praised by others. Truly, I say to you, they have received their reward. [3] But when you give to the needy, do not let your left hand know what your right hand is doing, [4] so that your giving may be in secret. And your Father who sees in secret will reward you.

The Lord's Prayer

[5] "And when you pray, you must not be like the hypocrites. For they love to stand and pray in the synagogues and at the street corners, that they may be seen by others. Truly, I say to you, they have received their reward. [6] But when you pray, go into your room and shut the door and pray to your Father who is in secret. And your Father who sees in secret will reward you.

[7] "And when you pray, do not heap up empty phrases as the Gentiles do, for they think that they will be heard for their many

words. ⁸ Do not be like them, for your Father knows what you
need before you ask him. ⁹ Pray then like this:

"Our Father in heaven,

hallowed be your name.

¹⁰ Your kingdom come,

your will be done,

on earth as it is in heaven.

¹¹ Give us this day our daily bread,

¹² and forgive us our debts,

as we also have forgiven our debtors.

¹³ And lead us not into temptation,

but deliver us from evil.

¹⁴ For if you forgive others their trespasses, your heavenly Father
will also forgive you, ¹⁵ but if you do not forgive others their
trespasses, neither will your Father forgive your trespasses.

Fasting

¹⁶ "And when you fast, do not look gloomy like the hypocrites,
for they disfigure their faces that their fasting may be seen by
others. Truly, I say to you, they have received their reward.

[17] But when you fast, anoint your head and wash your face,
[18] that your fasting may not be seen by others but by your Father who is in secret. And your Father who sees in secret will reward you.

Lay Up Treasures in Heaven

[19] "Do not lay up for yourselves treasures on earth, where moth and rust destroy and where thieves break in and steal, [20] but lay up for yourselves treasures in heaven, where neither moth nor rust destroys and where thieves do not break in and steal. [21] For where your treasure is, there your heart will be also.

[22] "The eye is the lamp of the body. So, if your eye is healthy, your whole body will be full of light, [23] but if your eye is bad, your whole body will be full of darkness. If then the light in you is darkness, how great is the darkness!

[24] "No one can serve two masters, for either he will hate the one and love the other, or he will be devoted to the one and despise the other. You cannot serve God and money.

Do Not Be Anxious

[25] "Therefore I tell you, do not be anxious about your life, what you will eat or what you will drink, nor about your body, what you will put on. Is not life more than food, and the body more than clothing? [26] Look at the birds of the air: they neither sow

nor reap nor gather into barns, and yet your heavenly Father feeds them. Are you not of more value than they? 27 And which of you by being anxious can add a single hour to his span of life? 28 And why are you anxious about clothing? Consider the lilies of the field, how they grow: they neither toil nor spin, 29 yet I tell you, even Solomon in all his glory was not arrayed like one of these. 30 But if God so clothes the grass of the field, which today is alive and tomorrow is thrown into the oven, will he not much more clothe you, O you of little faith? 31 Therefore do not be anxious, saying, 'What shall we eat?' or 'What shall we drink?' or 'What shall we wear?' 32 For the Gentiles seek after all these things, and your heavenly Father knows that you need them all. 33 But seek first the kingdom of God and his righteousness, and all these things will be added to you.

34 "Therefore do not be anxious about tomorrow, for tomorrow will be anxious for itself. Sufficient for the day is its own trouble.

MATTHEW 7

Judging Others

1 "Judge not, that you be not judged. 2 For with the judgment you pronounce you will be judged, and with the measure you use it will be measured to you. 3 Why do you see the speck that

is in your brother's eye, but do not notice the log that is in your own eye? [4] Or how can you say to your brother, 'Let me take the speck out of your eye,' when there is the log in your own eye? [5] You hypocrite, first take the log out of your own eye, and then you will see clearly to take the speck out of your brother's eye.

[6] "Do not give dogs what is holy, and do not throw your pearls before pigs, lest they trample them underfoot and turn to attack you.

Ask, and It Will Be Given

[7] "Ask, and it will be given to you; seek, and you will find; knock, and it will be opened to you. [8] For everyone who asks receives, and the one who seeks finds, and to the one who knocks it will be opened. [9] Or which one of you, if his son asks him for bread, will give him a stone? [10] Or if he asks for a fish, will give him a serpent? [11] If you then, who are evil, know how to give good gifts to your children, how much more will your Father who is in heaven give good things to those who ask him!

The Golden Rule

[12] "So whatever you wish that others would do to you, do also to them, for this is the Law and the Prophets.

[13] "Enter by the narrow gate. For the gate is wide and the way is easy that leads to destruction, and those who enter by it

are many. [14] For the gate is narrow and the way is hard that leads to life, and those who find it are few.

A Tree and Its Fruit

[15] "Beware of false prophets, who come to you in sheep's clothing but inwardly are ravenous wolves. [16] You will recognize them by their fruits. Are grapes gathered from thornbushes, or figs from thistles? [17] So, every healthy tree bears good fruit, but the diseased tree bears bad fruit. [18] A healthy tree cannot bear bad fruit, nor can a diseased tree bear good fruit. [19] Every tree that does not bear good fruit is cut down and thrown into the fire. [20] Thus you will recognize them by their fruits.

I Never Knew You

[21] "Not everyone who says to me, 'Lord, Lord,' will enter the kingdom of heaven, but the one who does the will of my Father who is in heaven. [22] On that day many will say to me, 'Lord, Lord, did we not prophesy in your name, and cast out demons in your name, and do many mighty works in your name?' [23] And then will I declare to them, 'I never knew you; depart from me, you workers of lawlessness.'

Build Your House on the Rock

[24] "Everyone then who hears these words of mine and does them will be like a wise man who built his house on the rock.

²⁵ And the rain fell, and the floods came, and the winds blew and beat on that house, but it did not fall, because it had been founded on the rock. ²⁶ And everyone who hears these words of mine and does not do them will be like a foolish man who built his house on the sand. ²⁷ And the rain fell, and the floods came, and the winds blew and beat against that house, and it fell, and great was the fall of it."

The Authority of Jesus

²⁸ And when Jesus finished these sayings, the crowds were astonished at his teaching, ²⁹ for he was teaching them as one who had authority, and not as their scribes.

NOTES

SERMON ON THE MOUNT

NOTES

LET'S BE FRIENDS!

BLOG

We're here to help you grow in your faith, develop as a leader, and find encouragement as you go.

lifewaywomen.com

SOCIAL

Find inspiration in the in-between moments of life.

@lifewaywomen

NEWSLETTER

Be the first to hear about new studies, events, giveaways, and more by signing up.

lifeway.com/womensnews

APP

Download the Lifeway Women app for Bible study plans, online study groups, a prayer wall, and more!

 Google Play App Store

Lifeway women

OTHER RESOURCES
by Jen Wilkin

ABIDE
10 Sessions

See how 1, 2, and 3 John call to Christians to recall a great salvation and abide in the truth.

lifeway.com/abide

BETTER
10 Sessions

Explore the book of Hebrews to learn how to place your hope and faith in Christ alone.

lifeway.com/better

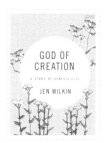

GOD OF CREATION
10 Sessions

Learn how the first 11 chapters of Genesis set the scene for the story of the Bible as a whole.

lifeway.com/godofcreation

GOD OF COVENANT
10 Sessions

Witness God's faithfulness in Genesis 12–50 to Abraham, Isaac, Jacob, and Joseph, and discern Christ in the stories of His people.

lifeway.com/godofcovenant

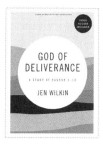

GOD OF DELIVERANCE
10 Sessions

Study Exodus 1–18 verse by verse to explore how God provided deliverance for His children to be able to worship Him freely and how it affects our lives today.

lifeway.com/deliverance

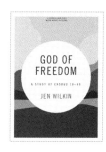

GOD OF FREEDOM
10 Sessions

Study Exodus 19–40 in depth to understand how the freedom God gives His children is meant to lead us to lives of glad service to God and our communities of faith.

lifeway.com/freedom

1 PETER
9 Sessions

Study the book of 1 Peter to look beyond your current circumstances to a future inheritance through Christ.

lifeway.com/1peterstudy

lifeway.com/jenwilkin | 800.458.2772

Lifeway women

Pricing and availability subject to change without notice.

Get the most from your study.

IN THIS STUDY YOU'LL:

- Gain a thorough understanding of Jesus's longest recorded message
- Study the Sermon on the Mount as a complete unit rather than in fragments
- Learn how a disciple of Jesus thinks, speaks, and acts

To enrich your study experience, consider the accompanying video teaching sessions from Jen Wilkin, approximately 40–60 minutes each.

STUDYING ON YOUR OWN?

Watch Jen Wilkin's teaching sessions, available via redemption code for individual video-streaming access, printed in this Bible study book.

LEADING A GROUP?

Each group member will need a *Sermon on the Mount* Bible study book, which includes video access. Because all participants will have access to the video content, you can choose to watch the videos outside of your group meeting if desired. Or, if you're watching together and someone misses a group meeting, they'll have the flexibility to catch up! A DVD set is also available to purchase separately if desired.

Browse study formats, a free session sample, video clips, church promotional materials, and more at

lifeway.com/sermononthemount